*H*ANGED*AT*
LINCOLN

S TEPHEN W ADE

The
History
Press

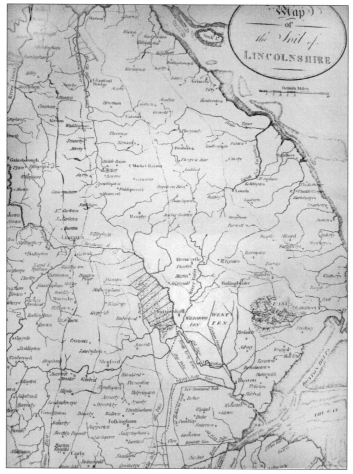

Map of Lincolnshire, from Arthur Young's Travels 1801.

First published 2009

The History Press
The Mill, Brimscombe Port
Stroud, Gloucestershire, GL5 2QG
www.thehistorypress.co.uk

Reprinted 2011, 2012

ISBN 978 0 7509 5110 4

Typesetting and origination by The History Press
Printed in Great Britain

CONTENTS

ACKNOWLEDGEMENTS

Crime history interests all kinds of writers and scholars, and sometimes enthusiasts whose names are little known provide the base for future writing. This certainly applies in the case of N.V. Gagen's self-published *Hanged at Lincoln 1716–1961*, which I have found invaluable. In addition, books by Adrian Gray and B.J. Davey (fully referenced in the bibliography) have been very useful.

Staff at Lincolnshire Archives, at the prison and castle sites, and at the Illustrations Index have been helpful. I have to thank Paul Kemp for his help with some Gainsborough references. Retired police officer Harry Johnson sent me helpful letters too.

Sources outside the normal archival records are notoriously difficult to assess, but crime historians rely on these ephemera for extra snippets of information and to complement known sources. In this respect, a chronicle written by a certain H. Capland in 1835 provided details of names and crimes, as did a list of executions at Lincoln published in *Ward's Historical Guide to Lincoln* (1880).

Thanks are due to the library staff in Lincoln public libraries who compiled cuttings books some years ago: these provided some aspects of social history that have helped enhance the narrative. The same applies to a number of pamphlets and journal articles, all listed in the bibliography. This was built on to some extent with scraps of oral history from staff at HMP Lincoln, where the last hanging (in 1961) has entered into history. The power of this for historians may be seen in Robert Douglas's book *At Her Majesty's Pleasure* (2007), in which he recalls sitting in the death cell with a condemned man in Bristol. I have been fortunate in that I have visited what was once the death cell in the Greetwell Road prison (before the refurbishment of A Wing) so I have my own small piece of historical testimony to add.

For details of the Belvoir witch case, I am indebted to the exemplary research carried out by Michael Honeybone. For permission to use the first page of the chapbook on that case, I must thank Magdalene College library, University of Cambridge.

For permission to reproduce the illustrations of the White Hart at Sibsey, and the White Horse at Market Deeping, thanks to the Local Studies Collection, Lincolnshire Archives, courtesy of Lincolnshire County Council.

Cassini Publishing Ltd kindly allowed reproduction of the map regarding Tom Otter.

Finally, thanks to the Lincoln Record Society for permission to use the illustration of the jurors' seals.

As to the nature of the tales told here: I have dealt with some of the more celebrated Lincolnshire hangings in more depth in my book *Lincolnshire Murders* (2006). In the present work, the aim is to provide a reference but also to produce more than a mere checklist of known facts. I have therefore omitted the cases of which we know very little from the main entries and listed them in the appendices.

INTRODUCTION

In 1843 the press reported a dreadful murder in Quadring, near Spalding; a schoolmistress named Mary Spencer was found in her cottage with her head almost severed from her body. Pupils arriving at the school had the horrendous sight of their teacher lying in a pool of blood. There was blood on the walls, and there had clearly been a struggle. As word spread, a labourer queried, 'I wonder what Bill's been up to? He was out all night and came in all over blood.'

The constable was called and William Howett was arrested. He was twenty-two and had been deaf and dumb since birth. An inquest was held at the Brown Cow Inn, where Howett's mother claimed she and the constable had gone to her son's room and found his shirt covered in blood. A committal warrant from the coroner directed Howett to be taken to Lincoln Prison. He was charged with wilful murder, but spared the hangman: instead he was committed to an asylum for the usual length of time in such cases – to be detained 'at her Majesty's pleasure'.

This case is not unusual. In spite of the popular narratives of murder in nineteenth-century England, and writings about children and young women being hanged, along with all kinds of petty offenders (by today's standards), the fact is that it would be easy to compile a book listing and describing those who killed other people in Lincolnshire in days gone by and yet did not hang. Even in the decades ruled by the Bloody Code of the eighteenth century, when there were 220 capital offences, the professionals in the law machine often did all they could to avoid giving the accused a date with the hangman. There were far fewer children hanged in the years before 1830, when capital offences began to reduce in number. Of course, in addition to the commutation of sentence to transportation or a prison term in England, there was the issue of the defence in court: potentially, that could reduce the number of hangings. But defences of insanity were difficult to apply successfully. Howett was fortunate in that respect, but his fate in the asylum was probably far from pleasant.

One of the most dramatic cases of reprieve was that of Priscilla Woodford, a farm servant who, in 1831, set fire to a haystack at Haconby where she worked, after a row with her employers. In the March 1832 Lincoln Assize she was sentenced to hang, at just sixteen years of age. In the early 1830s there was widespread rural crime, in the wake of what is now called the 'Swing Riots', and it must have looked as if Priscilla would hang. But a petition saw her sentence commuted to one of transportation to New South Wales, where she married a man who had also escaped the noose, Thomas Winstanley.

Lincoln has been a fortress and a place of prisons and scaffolds for many centuries. From Tudor times, there had been a courthouse and a county gaol within the castle walls; in the debtors' prison the chronicle shows that John Wesley's father was a debtor who spent time there. In contrast to the courthouse, which handled cases from Lincolnshire generally, Lincoln people were tried at the Guildhall in the Stonebow. The prison reformer, John Howard, saw the old prison when he prepared his great work of 1776, *The State of the Prisons*. The new prison within the castle was completed in 1787.

The prison as seen by the visitor today is primarily Victorian; William Lumley designed the interior and John Carr's famous design is evident in the exterior. Between 1846 and

The prison in the castle.
(Author's collection)

1848 the prison was enlarged, and in 1872 the new prison at Greetwell Road was built. From the death cells in the various gaols came the felons who were destined for the scaffold. The first gallows was close to what is now the small roundabout by the Burton road, close to the walls and the Struggler public house. The condemned felon would be taken there in a cart, and then the hangman would fit the noose over a crossbeam and let the horse go. In 1817 the Cobb Hall tower was used. The crowds who came to watch the criminals die could book a place in one of the taverns opposite and see the 'turning off' at the tower. Now that the trees have been cleared from the walls by Cobb Hall (in 2008) there is more of a sense of what the dramatic 'theatre of the scaffold' would have been like in terms of space and the vista of the death.

There were occasional escapes, such as by a man named Ralph. He escaped just before he was due to be transferred to Armley gaol in Leeds. He had a replica key and a way of escape through a coal cellar. Not long after this, in January 1855, there was an advertisement for a turnkey in the *Lincolnshire Times*. The salary was £40 a year and applications had to be in writing; part of the duties was to instruct the male prisoners in reading, writing and arithmetic.

Public hanging was abolished in 1868, and Priscilla Biggadike was the first victim at Lincoln to be privately hanged, out of view of the crowd, though reporters were present. By 1861, the number of capital sentences had been reduced to four: murder, attempted murder, treason and piracy in the dockyards. But the criminal law still had no appeal system for the poorer people: the courts of criminal appeal were not created

The Victorian prison, showing the view towards the execution route. (Author's collection)

The graves of executed killers. (Author's collection)

The prison, showing the wings. (Author's collection)

The Strugglers Inn, close to the Burton junction where the first gallows stood. (Author's collection)

until 1907. There was also a problem with the nature of manslaughter, notably in cases of infanticide and hiding a child – these were not included within manslaughter until 1922, and so some of the murder cases which were related to the killing of children through a number of economic reasons persisted as a problem throughout the century. In many cases, such affairs would mean that the women in question would be committed to an asylum.

In the twentieth century the steady move towards the abolition of the death penalty was marked by a series of committees and reports on all matters relating to hanging. In April 1948, hangings ceased for an experimental period of five years. From the 1870s, the Greetwell Road prison had been the place with the death cell, and now it was unused, until the last Lincoln hangings in the 1950s through to 1961. In March 1957 the Homicide Act was passed: murder was no longer automatically a capital offence once a new offence, 'capital murder', was created. There were six grades of capital murder and these are reflected in the last Lincoln hangings: murder in the furtherance of theft; murder by shooting or causing an explosion; murder in the course of escaping custody; the murder of police officers; the murder of prison officers, and a second killing tried at court. Despite this, Lincoln still had its reprieve dramas, as in the case of John Docherty in 1954. Docherty was legless, and had tried to take his own life – after murdering his fiancée – by hurling himself across the railway lines at Grantham. The Home Secretary exercised mercy; Docherty did not hang because of the clemency applied in relation to a physical deformity clause in the Homicide Act.

Mrs Van der Elst campaigning against hanging. (Author's collection)

This book covers the period between 1200 and 1961, but for reasons of space I have selected only a representative group of pre-1700 hangings. The fact is that there is little known about the earlier hangings. The period I have covered comprises four phases in the history of capital punishment in Britain. First, the Medieval to Stuart years were dominated by the 'Frank Pledge' and then the Curia Regis and the King's Bench courts; as the assizes developed, from the years of Henry I, execution gradually became more systematised in the new criminal justice procedure, rather than a matter of quick hangings carried out from a number of different courts (hence the number of 'gallows' references on early maps). Then, during the second phase, between the early Georgian period and around 1830, the Bloody Code dominated the scene. This is the term used to describe that period when there were so many capital crimes on the statute books. Up until 1800, about a third of condemned prisoners were actually hanged; one reason for this was the 1723 Black Act, mainly used to try to suppress poaching. The third phase was the period before the late 1860s, by which time public execution had ended and the number of capital crimes was reduced to four. Finally, the last century of hangings included a large number of issues, such as the training of hangmen (following a report of 1888) and the topics of diminished responsibility, hanging of children and the manslaughter/murder debate resolved.

Of hangings in the city before about 1700, there is little in the records, with a few exceptions, and I have listed these in the appendix. Some of those executions took place during times of great national furore, as was the case after the 1536 Pilgrimage of Grace, which had a prominent Lincolnshire following. In 1537 twelve men were tried at the Guildhall, including the Abbot of Barlings; all were hanged.

I have added an appendix in order to explain the Medieval and Early Modern legal system and the processes that led to hangings or otherwise, with a commentary on the lack of substantial detail of the material involved.

Reminder of the hangman's presence: Marwood's attic room was in this building. (Author's collection)

In earlier centuries, it is not possible to identify the hangmen at work in Lincoln. But from the early nineteenth century onwards we have some fairly substantial records. However, it is not until the famous and well-documented executioners; William Calcraft, James Berry, William Marwood, the Billingtons, Albert Pierrepoint, Steve Wade and Harry Allen, that we can add to the narratives of hanging at Lincoln with some biography of these men. Readers are referred to the books by Steve Fielding for this information.

Lincolnshire boasts the most innovative and humane of the famous hangmen; William Marwood was born in Horncastle and learned his trade, along with his advance in the use of the long drop, by hanging animals and bags of flour. James Berry, the Bradford hangman, carried out some work at Lincoln, including the hanging of Mary Lefley, of which he left a detailed account in his memoirs. In 1684, the notorious Judge Jeffreys came to the city, but as far as we know he did not hang anyone; at that time he was Lord Chief Justice.

Finally, it must be said that the legal and criminal history of the city is a factor in the tourist and heritage identity of Lincoln. It is a provoking experience to visit the castle, walk up the sharp slope to the Lucy Tower and see the sombre circle of gravestones belonging to executed felons beneath the trees, or to stand at the door of what was once the death cell and imagine the cries and despair of those about to die. What makes this experience yet more melancholy is the certainty that some of these unfortunates have since been proved innocent. The most prominent of these is Priscilla Biggadike. In the Lucy Tower we can still make out the initials 'P.B.' and the date, 1868. We know that she was innocent: Thomas Proctor confessed to the crime on his deathbed in 1882.

Not all murders ended in convictions of course, and the county is full of obscure and dramatic references to killings for which the perpetrator either did not hang or for which there was never an arrest. An example of this is a tombstone in the Sanctuary at St Mary's Church, Long Sutton, which bears the inscription 'Alas poor Bailey.' This refers to Dr John Bailey, a surgeon killed on the Tydd road on 21 April 1795, and whose murderer, Thomas Newman, was never caugh but confessed on the gallows (*see* chapter 49).

The Wig and Mitre, showing the connection with castle and assizes. (Author's collection)

Steps leading to the burial ground for felons. (Author's collection)

The entrance to the Lucy tower, burial place of the executed killers. (Author's collection)

1

WILLIAM KILLS WALTER

William Malbis, 1203

This case is included to give one example from very early criminal history, and a perusal of the assize rolls for Lincolnshire up to the end of the fifteenth century show just how rare it was for a hanging to be the sentence, given that there were so many acquittals. A potential felon was tried at the assize, usually in Lincoln if it was the Easter term, but for the other terms of the legal year, the accused were tried in London. Many ran out into outlawry, many paid fines and some were imprisoned.

Not all trials were held in criminal courts in the Middle Ages; many offences were tried in Church courts, but in Lincoln, unlike York for instance, there were very few hangings actually in the city – though it was different across the county, where there were plenty of gallows available.

But in the centuries before the justices of the peace and the system of gaol delivery, Lincolnshire hangings did take place. One early example was William Malbis of Gainsborough, whose story is brief. He killed one Walter Fulingaud, for which he was put into gaol at Lincoln, and then hanged. He was not tried at a higher court, and the punishment was done

The Seals of the Jurors on the Lincoln Roll. (Courtesy of the Lincoln Record Society)

in the frankpledge system – the earliest organised local justice system in England, whereby a community was responsible for an individual transgression, and in each tithing, when this was instituted in Anglo-Saxon times, the tithingman would ensure that a culprit was brought before a court leet to be tried. Walter was not: he was delivered for trial in Lincoln.

This first case illustrates how sketchy the details are of these early hangings. But the ominous words in Latin appear in the texts of the records: *suspensus fuit* – he was hanged.

2

A REGULAR VILLAIN

Walter Wright, April 1353

Fourteenth-century England suffered a widespread famine between around 1314 and 1319, and in addition to the foreign wars, there was the Black Death of 1348–9, when almost a third of the population died. There were gangs of desperate people and robberies were common. The Lincolnshire Peace Rolls for the years around the middle of the century show the most terrible crimes being committed in the county: in one example, four men broke into the house of a Thornton man, and raped and abducted his daughter. Their punishment? They were tried by the King's Bench in Lincoln and acquitted. So many crimes at the time were similarly atrocious, but hangings were few and far between. There were either no witnesses to the crime, or men who would speak for the accused in court, and it was a simple matter to walk free if the accused had any kind of social standing at all, though outlawry was common. Outlawry meant that the person was a felon and so would lose their land and chattels, as would their heirs. It was a huge punishment, but at least the criminal lived to fight another day.

However, Walter Wright, a servant working for William Carter in the parish of St Augustine, broke into the home of John Shipman and stole a chest belonging to a Boston man. He was tried before the very busy justice, William de Skipwith, and was sentenced to hang.

3

FOUR SENTENCED TO HANG

Margaret de Staindrop, Alan Taylor & others, April 1353

Along with Walter Wright (*see* previous chapter), who had to answer a charge of 'furtively stealing other goods valued at 40 shillings', were five others, and although one was

¶ The order and maner of burying in the Fields such as dyed in prison, and namely, of William Wiseman.

Burial of an Elizabethan felon. (Author's collection)

acquitted, four were hanged. The crimes were: stealing goods, including two oxen which were stolen in the Middle Fen and taken into Lincoln; the theft of a Maplewood bowl and four towels in a house; the theft of six ells of woollen cloth from a house; and other thefts from homes. The first reaction on reading this is the apparent unfairness: so many other cases at the time were for murder or rape, and yet these poorer folk were hanged for lesser offences. Margaret de Staindrop stole the brass pot and Alan Taylor took the ells of cloth. In the Peace Roll records we have the word 'suspensus' (hanged) repeated four times. A man named Edward was acquitted. William of Skipwith, the King's justiciar, was a busy man that day: in that office, he stood in place of the King when a trial took place without the sovereign himself being present.

The hangings were almost certainly carried out at what is now the small roundabout close to the Burton road. The culprit would stand in a cart and the horse slapped into action after the rope was tightened around their neck. Old illustrations show the rough and brutal methods, with religious men in attendance. The mystery will always be about the hangmen, however; until the Tudor period we have little information about the identities of the hangmen. The usual practice was for the hangman to be a convicted felon who saved his own neck by offering to do the deed.

3

4

A MURDEROUS PAIR

John Elmsall & Diota Baker, March 1396

Life was brutal and short for many during these perilous years, but this tale has nothing to do with famine or plague. It was simply a tale of removing the wife from the scene so that two lovers could be together. John Elmsall of Gainsborough and Diota, the wife of William Baker, chose the day before the Feast of St Andrew to make sure that John's wife would breathe no more. The record simply states that they 'came at night in the house of the said John Elmsall, murdered the wife of John, and fled as felons.'

The couple were arrested and taken to Lincoln to be tried at the Easter sittings for gaol delivery on 4 March 1395. As the Feast Day of St Andrew is on 30 November, and the hearing was the Easter Term, they probably spent a long time in the castle dungeon, as the gaol delivery and sentencing took place when the King's Bench sat, four times a year. We do not know the date of their arrest, but it is likely that they spent months in the gaol with the rats and disease. They would have been separated of course.

Both appeared before the coroner, were indicted and then sentenced to be hanged.

By the thirteenth century – an age of continental warfare – the king was in need of money, so fines were imposed, most commonly at this time when hanging was becoming the standard punishment, replacing mutilation and burning. As Andrew McCall has pointed out, Lincolnshire provides a typical example of this: '...out of a total of 317 cases [these were made up] of homicide (114), robbery (89), vagrancy (65), and rape (45), which the assize rolls for the years 1201–2 record as having been death with by the justices... 271 who were found guilty were fined, the sum of their fines amounting to 527.12s.' (The figures exclude those who fled, claimed immunity, or went to the Church court.) The killers in this case were hanged.

5

PUNISHED AFTER THE REVOLT

John Hussey & Richard Harrison, March 1537

The Pilgrimage of Grace of 1536, otherwise referred to in Lincoln as the Lincolnshire Rising, as it began in Louth, was a wide revolt against the religious and state practices of Henry VIII. As some of the smaller monasteries were dissolved, discontent spread, mainly in Lincolnshire and in Yorkshire – where Robert Aske was a major figure. The King responded by offering pardons if there was a reconciliation.

But savage reprisals followed and many of the leaders were hanged or beheaded. Of the Lincolnshire men, forty-six were tried in March 1537, but not all were hanged in Lincoln: some were taken to London, and one died in Camberwell. Thirty-one executions took place in Louth and Horncastle, but some major figures met their end in Lincoln itself. Most famous at the time was Lord Hussey of Sleaford. He was arrested and ordered to give full information about the rebellion.

John Hussey was attainted a traitor, and he pleaded that those to whom he was a debtor would not suffer by his forfeiture of possessions and title because of his attainder (an Act of Attainder took away all of a person's civil rights and privileges). Hussey was sixty-three years of age in 1529 when he gave evidence with regard to the marriage of Prince Arthur with Catherine of Arragon, so he was seventy when he was hanged. It was a terrible irony, as his father had been Lord Chief Justice in 1481. Hussey himself had been in Mary's household and wanted to restore the succession to her, but after Cromwell got to work on these matters, Hussey fell out of favour and his wife was imprisoned in the Tower for a while.

The other important figure who died in Lincoln was Richard Harrison, the Abbot of the Cistercian abbey, Kirkstead, a place that was already a ruin in 1913 when W.F. Rawnsley lamented: 'The ruinous state of this lovely little building which was used for public worship until Bishop Wordsworth prohibited it … has long been a crying scandal.' It was beautiful and in full use when Harrison was in charge, but after that fateful day in March 1537, he was never to return.

Harrison was arrested with three of his monks; at first the monks were bailed but in spite of some hope that there might be pardons, sentences of death on the monks followed and the monastery was attainted. The buildings were ruined and the other monks were told to go out into the world to beg, one assumes. However, there was apparently very little to plunder in the place, as Sir William Parr, who supressed a number of rebellions, reported.

6

TWO TRAITORS

Thomas Sprott & Thomas Hunt, 11 July 1600

Thomas Sprott and Thomas Hunt are considered 'venerable' in the Catholic Church. This means that they have reached the first of the three degrees of canonization, and are on their way to becoming saints. But they suffered horribly for their belief, and were hanged, drawn and quartered at Lincoln on 11 July 1600.

Sprott was born at Skelsmergh, Kendal, in Westmoreland, and was ordained a priest in Douai, at the English College, in 1596. He was soon sent on a mission and on 8 November 1598 he signed a letter to the Pope, supporting the archpriest in England – a major Catholic figure whose presence, of course, would be anathema to the Queen. He essentially signed his own death warrant.

Hunt, who originated from Norfolk, had been a student at the English College in Seville and had been ordained there. When he came to England on his mission, he was arrested and imprisoned at Wisbech, but he and some other men managed to escape just a few moths before he met with Sprott in Lincoln. While together at the Saracen's Head public house in Lincoln, the discovery of holy oils and some breviaries in their mail eventually condemned them. The trial was a travesty, with no real evidence against them, and it has been remarked that there was nothing to show that they were priests at all, but Sir John Glanville ordered that they should be found guilty.

They met their horrifying deaths with fortitude, but strange events were to follow: the judge who had tried them died just two weeks after their deaths, and later in July, John Glanville fell from his horse and died. He was a judge of the Common Pleas, and his instruction for the priests' deaths was one of his last actions.

7

THE BELVOIR WITCH CASE

Margaret & Phillipa Flower, 11 March 1619

In 1619, witch fever in Leicestershire had resulted in the hanging of nine women. When gossip turned to the Flower family in the Vale of Belvoir a short while later, the moral panic was accelerating. By the early months of 1619, two sisters, Margaret and Phillipa Flower, were being examined by magistrates, and in March they found themselves sitting before a Grand Jury.

Witchcraft was blamed by many on the troubles in the State and in the heart of the monarchy. James I had written on the subject, and there had been high-profile witch trials in many parts of the land. But what had the Flower sisters done? A pamphlet printed in London later in 1619 states that they were specially arraigned before the judges 'for confessing themselves actors in the destruction of Henry, Lord Rosse, with their damnable practices against others of the children of the Right Honourable Francis, Earle of Rutland.' The rest of the 'evidence' is a mix of gossip, sensation and distortion, such as stating that their mother, Joan, was 'a monstrous malicious woman'. They were supposed to have learned 'the manner of incantations, spells and charms' and then the son of the Rosse family, Henry, 'sickened very strangely and after a while died'.

Evidence was given by two women, Ann Baker and Joan Willimot, but the most informed writer on the subject, Michael Honeybone, is sure that the two sisters' own statements were what really condemned them. Although there is no record of what was actually said at the Lincoln trial, it seems right to assume that, as they had confessed under examination (although not tortured, as was the case in many other witch trials), and then accused each other, the justices were convinced that there had been attempts to communicate with the Devil.

Contrary to popular belief, 'witches' were not burned at the stake at this time. Women convicted of murdering their husbands were found guilt of Petit Treason, punishable by burning – as in the case of Eleanor Elsom in 1722 (see chapter 8). Witchcraft on the other hand was a felony, and was on the long list of offences punishable by hanging. The first Witchcraft Act was passed in 1542 and was soon repealed; then two Acts passed in 1563 and 1604 enforced harsher measures. But for most of the Middle Ages, because so many offences involved image-making and references to Satan, witchcraft was defined specifically as 'calling forth Satan'.

Cobb Hall, the hanging tower. (Author's collection)

Across the border in Scotland, and on the continent, the Flower sisters would have been burned to death. In Lincoln they were walked to Cobb Hall, Lincoln Castle, and hung.

8

BURNED AT THE STAKE

Eleanor Elsom, 20 July 1722

Few events in the history of crime can equal the punishment for women who were condemned for murdering their husband. Such was the barbarity of this punishment that, in many cases, the family and friends of the victim tried to find a way to ensure that death occurred before the fire was lit.

During the early eighteenth century, men were considered more valuable in law than women. So if a woman killed her husband, she was guilty not merely of murder but the much more serious crime of Petit Treason. Petit Treason was defined by the Treason Act of 1351 and was the betrayal of a superior by a subordinate. The punishment for a man convicted of Petit Treason was to be drawn to the place of execution and hanged, but not quartered as in the case of High Treason. However the punishment for a woman was to be burned at the stake, the same penalty as for High Treason. This continued into the early nineteenth century, when campaigners such as the energetic and humanitarian Samuel Romilly campaigned to reform the criminal law of England.

But in Lincolnshire in 1722, Eleanor Elsom was convicted of taking her husband's life and sentenced to die. She was taken from her cell and fastened upon a hurdle of wood, her body having been tarred. A rope was then tied around her neck and her body tightly bound to the stake. She would not be able to move when the fire was lit. There is no evidence that Eleanor was given a merciful death before the flames consumed her, but it is hoped that she was spared this agony.

This punishment was abolished in 1790 and substituted by hanging. But in Eleanor Elsom's days, the stake was waiting for such felons.

9

ROBBER BROTHERS

Isaac & Thomas Hallam, March 1733

Isaac and Thomas Hallam spent their lives moving between Lincoln and London. Isaac started his working life as a post boy in Lincoln when he was just twelve; but later, the young man was in the debtor's prison, put there by a Mr Rands. The resulting hatred from that imprisonment was to be the beginning of a path to infamy – so much so that the brothers provide one of the few Lincolnshire stories that made it into the famous *Newgate Calendar* of crime stories. After failing in business in London, the two brothers crossed the line into criminality and began to earn a living as highway robbers.

The brothers' crime spree covered a very large area: most of the East of England, from Epping to Lincolnshire, felt their mark. They robbed both on foot and on horseback in various places. But in January 1733 they were in Dunholme, just a few miles north of Lincoln. There they joined up with a man named William Wright. After a few drinks, the three men left together for Market Rasen, going through Faldingworth. It was a perfect opportunity for the Hallams to make some easy money. They simply had to rob Wright, as he was in his cups (extremely drunk). At first they failed and he took off, but later, at Ings Gate, they met him again and there they killed him by cutting his throat. At Holton Beckering they drank again, and soon came across a post boy, Thomas Gardiner. At this time, the mail was transported across the land between relay-points, and the carts were supposed to move at six miles an hour. Of course these post boys, who were not armed, were easy prey for highwaymen; it was often argued that they were in league with robbers as it was such a profitable crime.

But in this case young Thomas, just nineteen years of age, had his throat cut, and never reached his destination of Langworth. The Hallams waited for the postmaster, who they

Nettleham Church, where one of the robbers was buried. (Author's collection)

thought would also come along, but he did not. They went off with 25s and some food. They returned south and went to work around London again, but news of the murder was out and a handsome reward advertised. They were duly arrested and taken to Lincoln. Outside the city, the local post boys gathered to blow their horns as the killers were brought to gaol.

In March, at the Lent assizes, the Hallams were tried before Mr Justice Probyn, who had just sat at the infamous Princess Serafina trial in London, at which the crime of sodomy was much publicised. Probyn sentenced the two brothers to hang. Isaac was hanged at Nettleham, just north of Lincoln, and his body gibbeted at the scene as was the custom; his brother was hanged at Faldingworth, where his corpse was also gibbeted. As N.V. Gagen has pointed out, the dates of the hangings are uncertain. The *Newgate Calendar* states that they were hanged on 20 February, but contemporary reports say 22 March and also 23 March. Whatever the exact date, justice was done and the post boys had their revenge. The memorial in Nettleham preserves the memory of their barbarity and the severe justice done.

10

A BURGLAR AND A ROBBER

Thomas Dixon & William Marshall, 17 March 1738

Mr Justice Comyns had a burglar and a highway robber standing before him in court. Comyns was to be appointed Chief Baron of the Exchequer just a few months after this trial, from 1667 to 1740, and was a controversial character, having been accused of refusing to take the Qualification Oath when standing for Maldon in 1715.

The facts of the case are few, but it is known that Thomas Dixon had forced an entry into the house of a certain John Lacey. Not satisfied with simply robbing the place, he then proceeded to set the property on fire. He walked out with £6 12s. His offences were against the basic tenets of citizens' rights to peace and property.

Equally, William Marshall had robbed the Gainsborough mail, so his offence was against the Crown and People, and reprieves for highway robbery were few. Marshall had a history of criminal activity, so there was no hope of his neck being saved.

A succession of statutes at this time increased the range of crimes that resulted in capital punishment. This included appearing in armed groups with blackened faces (an offence under the 1723 Black Act, so called because it was passed in response to an outbreak of poaching committed by men who disguised themselves by 'blacking' their faces). All this increased the general fear of crimes committed at night – so burglary was seen as an extreme offence in any context.

Both men were destined for the gallows, and they met their end on 17 March 1738. As for the powerful Sir John Comyns, he had not long to live either, he died at Writtle in July 1740.

11

DICK TURPIN'S TRADE

William Lomax, Thomas Sharp & Joseph Binge, 23 March 1739

When these felons stood in the courtroom in Lincoln, the infamous Dick Turpin was in gaol at Beverley, just a month away from his death – he was executed on the York Knavesmire in April. One of his many crimes was horse-stealing – a capital offence and viewed very seriously. Ironically, Turpin's story has a strong connection with Lincolnshire because his horse-stealing trade happened largely in the south of the county, at Heckington, and he would sell his horses in East Yorkshire. But William Lomax and Thomas Sharp, who practised that same dangerous trade, were in no way as celebrated as Turpin.

At the Lent assizes in March 1739 they stood with Joseph Binge, a housebreaker, before Mr Justice Page and Baron Thompson. Lomax had been running his criminal trade between Lincolnshire and Derbyshire and had done well financially. But it was a high-risk affair and he had soon been tracked down. Incredibly, the very young Thomas Sharp admitted that he had stolen eighteen horses. It was not a difficult offence to commit. Later, at the end of the century, many were transported to Van Dieman's Land for the crime, but in the repressive 1730s it was a trade that usually led to the scaffold, as it did for Sharp and Lomax.

As with Thomas Dixon (see chapter 10), Joseph Binge had broken into a home and he too had to pay the maximum penalty.

12

A LANCASHIRE MAN MURDERED

Philip Hooton, March 1769

Fustian was a standard material worn by the working man in the Georgian and Victorian years; it was basically a mixture of cotton and linen, with a soft surface. In 1841, the Chartist, Feargus O'Connor, wrote in his newspaper that he was appealing to 'the fustian jackets, the unshorn chins and the blistered hands' of the working man. The twilled material was soft and called at times 'poor velvet', but there was nothing poor about the men who made and sold it.

Such a man was Lancashire businessman Samuel Stockton, who came from Astley. When he came to see the corn markets in the Fen country, Stockton was unfortunate enough to meet Philip Hooton, who was operating as a conman, with the front of a travelling preacher. He was so skilled at his nefarious craft that he gained his victim's confidence to such a degree that Stockton was willing to raise money for the purchase of corn in Lincolnshire; the plan being to transport it and sell it at a profit in Lancashire.

The two men were companions, but as they walked out together by the banks of the Welland, near Surfleet, Hooton set about Stockton and murdered him, clearly with the intent of robbing him. Before a jury, Hooton tried to claim that he never meant to kill the Lancashire man, but it was to no avail. In keeping with his mock-religious public image, the killer called on his Saviour to help him, but he was destined to be hanged and gibbeted; most likely being hanged in Lincoln and then his body being taken to the gibbet at the scene of the killing, as was the usual custom.

13

A KILLING IN GAOL

William Matthews, March 1770

In 1769, a brutal murder took place in Lincoln Castle Gaol that was entirely in keeping with the kind of terrible violence we find in criminal fraternities in most hard times in history. In this case the victim was a sheep-stealer named Lusby, who was attacked and killed by one of the most ruthless and amoral men in these annals – William Matthews. Matthews teamed up with another villain, who was part of a gang supposedly 'grassed' by

Lusby, and the two men killed their victim by breaking his ribs and so causing a puncture to his heart.

For serious crimes (felonies) the prisoners had to wait in gaol until the next assizes (the justices would arrive at the courts twice a year), and so Matthews was tried at the Spring assizes in 1770. He and his accomplice had already made it clear that they should 'die with pleasure.' There was no doubt about the judicial outcome; but it was at this point that the true depths of Matthew's iniquity came to light. He confessed to a terrible crime at Normanby – the poisoning of three members of the Cooke family, and a woman named Elizabeth Emerson, by putting arsenic in the butter.

So bold was the killer that he put in a request to the judges: after being sentenced to hang by Mr Justice Aston, 'he desired his Lordship' to arrange matters so that he could be executed early, and so 'dine with the devil at noon.' The justice was ready to oblige and Matthews was hanged, though on what specific date in March is not clear as records and reports disagree.

We do not know how he died, but from the tone and attitude of the few reported words of the man, he surely gave the crowd 'a good death' in the sense that he went with fortitude and a touch of drama.

14

BAYONETED TO DEATH

James Kearney, August 1770

Life in the Georgian army was certainly tough, and it was full of criminals; desperate men running from bastardy claims, legal prosecution, gambling debts, and feuds. The average soldier was tough, hardy and cared little for human life. Such a man was James Kearney, a dragoon serving in a regiment called Bland's. In some respects, this was a distinguished regiment; it had served England well at the battle of Dettingen in 1743, where a soldier named Thomas Brown had been knighted by the King after showing conspicuous bravery. But there was little of that quality in Private James Kearney.

In Boston, in July 1770, Kearney spent the night drinking a great deal of liquor with a Friskney man. What happened next is tragically familiar – the two men continued drinking into the early hours of the morning, at which time the Friskney man went to sleep in the same room as Kearney, but the latter took out his bayonet and stabbed his victim many times in a frenzy of blood-lust. Not satisfied with the stabbing, the soldier then battered the poor man with the blunt end of the weapon, before leaving him to die.

In a mad rage, he then went to the room the landlady occupied, most likely in search of another victim, but people soon arrived on the scene and took him prisoner. He was consequently taken to Lincoln, and the only thing he could say was that he was thirsting for blood and that, 'I would have more if it was in my power.'

Today, we may well attribute his actions to post-traumatic stress, brought on through warfare. However his previous military experience is unknown to us and the only record we have suggests a man who was extremely violent when full of alcohol. Kearney died on the gallows in August 1770.

15

CAUGHT AT THE SWAN

John Lyon, 24 March 1775

Highway robbery was booming in the last decades of the eighteenth century. It was in those years that villains on the road, looking for easy takings, were rife in open commons or on the main routes of established roads. It was also a time when turnpikes were on the increase, but paying a fee for a well-kept stretch of road was no guarantee of safety. There were still no efficient forces of preventative law at work across the land, and travellers were wise to move about in groups.

A Frampton man named John Thorpe was on a turnpike road in Wyberton when John Lyon stopped and robbed him. Thorpe, however, then recruited a friend to go with him and apprehend the robber. The two pursuers caught up with Lyon at the Swan Inn at Sibsey. The highwayman had every intention of shooting Thorpe and it was only by the intervention of the landlord that he did not have the chance to do it. The robber was detained and searched; he had done very well, having over sixteen guineas on him, and also a gold watch. He clearly saw that he was outnumbered. Gaol in Lincoln was his destiny, and then the rope.

Baron Eyre was the judge, a man who showed mercy a few years later when he arranged the reprieve of a condemned teenager in Norfolk. But he had no mercy for this culprit and sentenced him to death. Just a few months later, Eyre himself had to suffer a death much closer to him – his daughter Mary drowned whilst crossing the Irish Sea in November of the same year.

16

A CASE OF MATRICIDE

William Farmery, 4 August 1775

There are few historic murder cases in Lincolnshire which feature the killing of a mother. Yet such was the case of William Farmery in Sleaford, who murdered his mother, Elizabeth, on 25 May 1775.

He was just twenty-one and wanted a lie-in. His mother dutifully reprimanded him for his laziness and he eventually got out of bed. But there was murder in his heart. He was told to bring a bucket of water in, and indeed he went outside, but sharpened his knife instead, then came back in, grabbed his mother and stabbed her in the neck, mortally wounding her.

Covered in her blood, William took off his incriminating coat and ran off, but in his panic he was observed: women servants saw the blood on him, and the hunt was then on for him. His poor father was the first to find Elizabeth's corpse.

When apprehended and questioned, William claimed that he had been planning the murder for three years; he said that he had endured years of being put down by his mother and was tired of her constant disciplining. The facts suggest that he had experienced failure in life, and had consequently felt a deep bitterness inside him. His laziness had meant that he never made a success of being an apprentice shoemaker in Leasingham. He had tried other work, but had been desultory.

William Farmery very likely did not want to leave his bed on the morning of 4 August 1775 either – as it was to be his last walk to the noose.

17

A CRIME SPREE

James Lee, 21 March 1777

The value of the goods stolen from the home of a certain William Hanly in Swineshead in early October 1776 was the huge sum (at the time) of £50. The man who managed to pull this off was a pathological thief, James Lee. In that period of English legal history, such a large sum would ensure that a felony had been committed – something way beyond the everyday crime of larceny. Often, juries would accept a lowered value of goods stolen if the accused was in dire poverty, but in this case Lee had clearly been on a crime spree.

The list of his offences was long: he had stolen goods in Boston, Stow Green and Swineshead. From Boston he had taken goods worth £7 from a shop and had stolen material from a booth at Stow Green. What was worse, he had forcefully entered the premises of William Turner and there had taken more property, this time to the value of £10.

Lee stood before Mr Justice Nares, and there was no doubt what the outcome would be. The thief was to hang. Nares, from Stanwell in Middlesex, had a reputation for wit and humour; he was vastly experienced and practised at the bar at Common Pleas until 1784. A colleague once called him 'the quintessential common lawyer'. This man of feeling and wide learning had to don the black cap that day, and there was no following letter recommending commutation. Lee went to the scaffold on 21 March 1777. The more we reflect on what the judges of assize had to do, and so frequently in the last decades of the eighteenth century and in the Regency, the more it has to be appreciated just what most of them needed in terms of fortitude and resolve to sentence so many to the ultimate punishment.

18

FAMILY MURDERED

Henry Atkinson, 18 July 1777

The occurrence of infanticide is sad enough, but often the means of death was a terrible one, usually through asphyxia or poison. Tragically, it was far more brutal in this case.

Henry Atkinson claimed in court that he had not known his wife was pregnant when they wed, and, furthermore, there was no evidence that the baby was his. On discovery, his wrath was taken out on the child. He took the babe from its bed and used his knees as a vice on its head, crushing its skull and leaving it die.

At the inquest, Atkinson was named the culprit and charged with wilful murder. He was convicted at the summer assizes on 12 July 1777 by the great Mr Justice Blackstone, the

An image of infanticide from a contemporary print. (Author's collection)

author of *Commentaries on the Laws of England*, and was hanged just six days later, on 18 July. It seems ironic that such a famous man should pass sentence on such a horrendous crime, largely because our image of him is mainly of a scholarly, academic type, not a man of everyday law practice. He surely recalled that time in Lincoln when he reflected later upon his career.

19

FOOTPAD HANGED

Thomas Hamm, 25 July 1777

The year 1777 was a busy one for the judges and hangmen of Lincolnshire. In this case it was yet another highway robbery. On 8 May 1777 Thomas Hamm and his accomplice, William Allen, robbed William Speight near Bourne, close to the signpost at Morton. They stole a yellow canvas purse containing three and a half guineas. It took a very short time to apprehend them at a tavern not far away, at Dembleby, Grantham.

The two robbers were footpads; hiding near a crossroads so that when travellers stopped they could be easily attacked, even though they might be on horseback and the attackers on foot.

The trial led to both robbers being sentenced to death, but there was an important difference in the criminal careers of the two men that saved the life of Allen. Hamm had a record and had in fact been sentenced to death before, at the Lent assizes the previous year, but had been reprieved. He had also previously been sent to a hulk on the Thames, but had escaped and returned to his home county to steal again. There was to be no third chance for him this time: Allen's life was spared, but Hamm was sent to the gallows.

20

HIGHWAYMEN AT GRANTHAM

Edward Dodson & Robert Blades, 20 March 1778

On 29 November 1777 highwayman Edward Dodson put his pistol to the head of Henry Bates, an Ancaster butcher, and said, 'Your money – or you are a dead man directly.' He stole gold and silver from the man.

Dodson and Robert Blades were working together with a determination that was going to raise mayhem that night. They went on and looked for more victims, and found one in Michael Matkin from Fulbeck. What happened when Matkin tried to run from them showed the butcher how wise he had been to accept the situation and part with his valuables, because Matkin was shot dead and left to run on, dead on his horse. That meant that other travellers were present and the poor man was consequently never robbed by the villainous pair.

The two robbers had been so bold that the countryside was in arms against them and in pursuit. A hue and cry was raised and the two men were caught at Bisbrooke the day after the attacks.

Lord Chief Baron Skynner and Mr Justice Ashurst sentenced the two men to death, but in their defence, Dodson tried to argue that he had not intended to kill Mtakin, that it had been an accident. They also claimed to have released another potential victim that night, without harm or robbery.

The defining moment of this particular case is that Blades refused to die on the scaffold while wearing his boots. As the rope was placed around his neck, he took them off, thus defying the old adage of 'dying with your boots on'.

21

FORGER AND THIEF DIE TOGETHER

Edward Johnson & Jonathan Barnet, 15 March 1782

Forgery of the King's coin was a very serious business and, in Regency England, usually led to the noose. There were networks of forgers across the land, notably between the West Country and Hull, in the early nineteenth century, and in the West Riding of Yorkshire there had been the notorious Cragg Vale coiners in the late eighteenth century.

Forgery covers various types of crime – making a false document, signature or note is most common, but also with 'an intent to fraud and deceive.' After the arrival of paper currency in 1694 there were then new varieties of forgery to consider. Between the Bank Act of 1697 and the year 1727, there were 618 death sentences given in Britain for committing forgery.

Edward Johnson forged some bills of exchange in 1781 to the value was £10. As the names of some endorsers were on the bills, so the indictment on him was worded to define what he aimed to do: 'having uttered and published the same as true knowing it to be forged with intent to defraud William Martindale of Gainsborough.' He was arrested, charged and sent to Lincoln Castle to await trial at the Lent assizes in 1782.

As for Jonathan Barnet, he stole a black mare – a crime which often resulted in a life sentence with transportation, but the value of this animal was £5, and the seriousness of the offence meant that sixty-year-old Barnet was sent to the gallows.

Both men were hanged on 15 March 1782. Such retribution for what must have seemed to many a minor offence must surely have made people think twice.

The assize court, Lincoln.
(Author's collection)

22

A CASE OF ARSON

John Storey, 2 August 1783

Arson was an offence that struck terror into the citizens of Britain in the days before a professional police force existed; it still does so now, of course, but imagine a society in which essentially one's own family was the best provider of security and reprisal for many. But on top of that, offences against property were such that the wealthier citizens would have to do something to instil fear into any poorer folk with a grudge. Arson was often an act done in vengeance, when a servant had been sacked for instance.

Statistics for the years 1814–1834 show that there were 215 convictions for arson in England; of these, eighty-seven felons were actually hanged. The rest would have been transported to the colonies. What was happening was that, if a felon was out of the country, thousands of miles across the seas, then he was highly unlikely to be a threat to property here again. So after the turn of the eighteenth century, when more felons were sent to Australia (after the loss of the American colonies), the number of hangings for arson declined.

All this is very relevant to the case of John Story, because he set fire not only to his own house, but that of his neighbour, Mr Tabor, of Market Deeping. It may have been accidental, but the court decided that it was intentionally done. Storey's cries that he was innocent did him no good at all, and Lord Chief Justice Loughborough sentenced him to hang at the assizes in July 1782. The record shows that the man launched himself into eternity, before the hangman could do his sombre business.

23

COINERS HANGED

Edward Perplar & William Dale, 22 August 1783

Sometimes, the potential profits of engaging in coining – known as 'the yellow trade' – were so tempting that gangs worked out ways of operating on a contained level, moving around within a circumscribed area. But the work of some magistrates in other parts of the country had shown the legal establishment that it was possible to track down the gangs, with a little resolution and some smart thinking.

That is what happened to Edward and Eleanor Perplar and William Dale in July 1783. They answered a knock at their door in Leicester and were arrested. They had coined shillings and sixpences in Grantham. The culprits were taken under guard back to Grantham and, by 28 July, were in Lincoln Castle.

Eleanor Perplar was acquitted, but the two men were convicted of coining: they had made fifteen pieces of metal into counterfeit currency. Unusually, they did not walk to the gallows, but were put on hurdles and dragged to the place of execution. The purpose of

The Angel at Grantham.
(Author's collection)

this indignity was to show the need for deterrence to all present. The brief report noted that they were 'affected by their melancholy fate', which normally meant that something of a devout nature had been spoken at the scaffold, where a clergyman would say a prayer with them before the noose was fitted.

24

FOUR DIE ON THE SCAFFOLD

Thomas Wood, Richard Dowind, William Davison & Richard Bull,
18 March 1784

The crimes in question here were burglary, committed by Thomas Wood, Richard Dowind and William Davison, and sheep-stealing by Richard Bull. In the latter case, Bull was just twenty-five years old, a Frampton man with convictions for other thefts, who had stolen seven sheep at Kirton. He had foolishly asked a neighbour to temporarily keep them for him. This action was unusual; as such offenders were often desperately poor men who stole sheep in order to feed a hungry family. As one writer said in 1781, 'Poverty alone can induce men to be guilty of sheep-stealing, and it is very hard that the same severity should be inflicted on the wretched sheep-stealer... as upon the hardened highwayman who robs to support himself in luxuries'. In Bull's case, the theft was committed for profit rather than through desperation, with nothing of the manner of the old song:

> Then I'll ride all around in another man's ground,
> And I'll take a fat sheep for my own,
> Oh I'll end his life with the aid of my knife,
> And then I will carry him home.

Bull was clumsy to say the least: the sheep he left with the neighbour had identifying marks on them. As for the three burglars: Wood broke into a house at Saxilby and stole a silver tankard and some money. He had done the job with some accomplices who had not been traced; the housewife had been disturbed by the noise and awoke to find Wood in the house, who subsequently threatened her and her husband with violence. After the villains' escape, it took only a week to trace them and they were duly arrested.

Dowind and Davison stole objects and cash from a house in Langrick Ferry. Their haul included the very large sum of £20. But the thieves were caught trying to sell the booty in Boston. They gave some tall tale about some other men burying the goods, but all to no avail and they found themselves in court before Baron Eyre on 10 March. What made things worse for the felons was that Bull and Davison had tried to escape some weeks before the trial. There was no question of mercy after that, even though Davison had a pregnant wife.

This is a particularly interesting case because a printed broadsheet gives details of the hangings. Many of these have not survived, as they were ephemeral printings, but we know from this one that 'they mounted the steps with great fortitude, acknowledged themselves guilty of the crimes for which they suffered, and begged the spectators to be warned by their untimely end.' There was also a moment of drama when two young men who had been reprieved for horse-stealing actually walked up to place the ropes and caps on the condemned. This was an extra piece of ritual, not often performed, in which the nature of a reprieve was highlighted for all present. We read that '… the young men descended and the trembling offenders, calling upon the Saviour of the World to receive them… left suspended by the neck until they were dead.'

25

A VICIOUS ATTACK

Richard Dennis & William Wright, 7 August 1784

The 1780s was a decade of executions in Lincoln: a relentless succession of felons being led from the death cell to the scaffold. The local reporters were never short of sensational copy. But although many cases were pathetic and desperate, the crime of Richard Dennis must have seemed unusually violent, even for those hard times.

Dennis was a highwayman who robbed and attacked John Stanny at Holbeach on 17 June 1784. He stole money, but also beat up his victim in a frenzied attack. He was caught and was in Lincoln a month later.

William Wright, in contrast, was a thief of many names and guises who was finally apprehended after stealing some linen and woollen cloth from a carrier named Daubray of New Sleaford. The interesting footnote here is that the goods were in a wagon when they were stolen – so was that housebreaking? It is not clear what actually led the case to a death sentence, as there were two offences – he also stole from the Pack House at Key Wharf.

There is some confusion as to when these two men were actually hanged, as some records say it was 1787. However, they were at trial in 1784, and there is no known reason why there should be a period of three years before sentence was carried out.

26

A HANGING AND AN ACQUITTAL MYSTERY

Patience Elsom, November 1784

In the chronicles of late Georgian trials, it is noticeable there were quite a few cases in which a man was reprieved and a woman executed for the same offence. I have written elsewhere of a similar case in Beverley in 1799. In that case, which involved a child-murder after extreme brutality by two women and a man; the man was acquitted and the two women executed for the crime, although why remains a mystery.

This is a similar case – that of Patience Elsom. She and her husband Robert stood accused of arson, charged with burning a wagon belonging to William Goulding in Ingoldsby on 18 July 1784. Patience was sentenced to hang, but Robert was acquitted. We can only speculate why this should be. Perhaps the man was a debtor and the creditors would have no money from a corpse. Or was there a separate argument for both? Unfortunately, there is no written record. The most cynical interpretation is that Robert had powerful friends. Whatever the details, all we have is the outcome.

27

NINE DIE AFTER SPRING ASSIZE

John Huson, William Holdworth, Thomas Rawson, John Palferman, William Ligburn & others, 18 March 1785

Multiple hangings were not unusual in England at this time, but six in one go was still a lot. Three of the executed were sheep-stealers, which was often a poor man's crime. In 1800 a sheep in Lincolnshire was worth an average of 35s, while wool in Lincoln brought around nine pence.

Among the felons were John Huson, highway robber; William Holdworth, horse-stealer; Thomas Rawson, burglar; John Palferman, who stole beasts; and William Ligburn, who committed a street robbery. They and four others (two more were later reprieved) were all sentenced to die at the Lent assizes of 1785, before Mr Justice Heath. Huson was arguably the worst offender, as he robbed a Mr Holmes of guns, silver and a bag, late at night in June 1784. Rawson was the boldest: he took gold, silver, shoe buckles, and a large amount of gold from two houses, one in Bonby and one in Castlethorpe. Ligburn robbed a man close to the White Hart Inn, absconding with gold and silver.

An attempt at escape by several of the condemned men added drama to the story. The outcome was a scrap involving soldiers as well as people from the debtors' prison who had learned of the escape attempt. Ironically, one of the condemned, a man named Harrison, raised the alarm, but it did his cause no good at all.

A crowd of 20,000 were present when the felons were hanged. Harrison said to the spectators, 'There is many here who knows my parents. I beg it a favour that they will cast no reflections on them. For had I took their advice… I should never have come to the gallows.'

The White Hart, Sibsey.
(Lincolnshire Archives)

A multiple hanging. (Drawing by Laura Carter)

28

AN IDENTITY PROBLEM

John Smith & Thomas Golling, 29 July 1785

As with the famous killer Tom Otter (*see* chapter 57), the John Smith of this case was also an alias: he was really Richard Carpenter, although his true name was not revealed until after his execution. He was convicted of stealing a mare from a certain George Kennington in Wrawby. As previously noted, judges and magistrates of the day took a dim view of horse-stealing, and Smith was sentenced to die.

As for Thomas Golling, he was a burglar, and he teamed up with a man named Thompson to rob a house at Sutterton, where they stole dresses and money. For reasons unknown, Thompson's life was spared, but Golling was sentenced to hang. In many cases of this period, the record is sparse, and no reason for the acquittal is forthcoming. Golling was a militiaman, and, as noted in other cases, it looks as though militiamen were frequently up before the judge. After all, they would have money for drink and time on their hands at some points of the year.

There is a report of the hanging and it was ostensibly more stoical than entertaining for the crowd. Crowds at executions often expected either a defiant speech or a holy one. In this instance the report indicates that Golling was even playful, winking at the crowd as he walked to the gallows. But the writer at the time stresses the perfunctory nature of the events: 'They neither addressed the spectators to take warning nor were observed to supplicate for pardon and mercy at the throne of grace.'

29

MURDER OF A BABY SON

Joseph Wilkinson, 16 March 1786

Mercury at this time was in the form of a salt and was the fatal substance chosen by twenty-three-year-old illiterate Joseph Wilkinson to end the life of his baby son. The killer from Wigtoft stood accused at the Lent Assizes in 1786, with Mr Justice Heath ready to sentence him. The court were told that the accused had placed a quantity of mercury into the child's mouth. It was a brutal and callous act, and a case of wilful murder.

The deed was done one Sunday in the previous year; the young man knew that the child was upstairs and said he was going up to change his shirt. His wife allowed the child to sleep on, but then later, when it was feeding time, she went to the child and saw what were described as lumps of mercury on the neck. A doctor was called but could do nothing, and the baby died a few days later – a long and painful death.

Records reveal that Wilkinson had had homicidal tendencies before this date, and had previously tried to kill his wife.

The rogue knew that he was doomed and ran off into the countryside. After a long and determined search for him, he was caught and imprisoned. There was never going to be any other sentence than death, and he was hanged on 16 March. Questions surrounding his mental health were not raised, for in 1786 such considerations were deemed unnecessary except in cases where the insanity was clear for all to observe.

30

SHEEP-STEALERS DIE

Henry Knowles & Stephen Tarr, 24 March 1786

Such was the fear of .rural crime at this time that groups of landowners and farmers began to organise societies for the prosecution of felons: they would act as detectives and constables where necessary, and it became a kind of neighbourhood-watch scheme. They were vulnerable because their lands were often extensive and it was very expensive to patrol all the fences. At night, of course, they were particularly open to theft.

In the period between 1771 and 1779, there were eighty-two cases of sheep-stealing at the Lincoln assizes. Thirteen of these resulted in death sentences, though some of these were reprieved. Other punishments were rare: only one of these felons was whipped, and two elected to join the army. Four were transported.

Many thefts of animals were never solved, so the need to deter other would-be thieves was high when some were caught. In this case, Henry Knowles and Stephen Tarr stole three ewes at Whaplode and a cow at Langtoft respectively. Knowles was only eighteen, but that was no excuse for leniency on the part of the judge, Mr Justice Heath, and both men were hanged.

31

ONE DIES, ONE HANGS

John Curtis, 12 May 1786

John Curtis and Paul Page robbed the home of a certain Mr Gascoign in Surfleet. They took the large sum of money of £40. Their appearance at the Lent assizes saw them both sentenced to die. But this case raises the interesting issue of respites. At this time, a judge could call for a respite to be considered – in fact it was on a point of law, and he made the decision just a day before they were due to hang. But Mr Justice Heath applied this only to Page. We do not know what the point of law was, but the interesting aspect of this is what it shows about the system.

A felon could be pardoned after the sitting of the so-called 'Hanging Cabinet' in London, after the creation of the Home Office in 1782; but equally, a circuit judge could call for a respite and take advice from colleagues. The group of judges would decide on whether a commutation of the sentence was to be done. Luck was on Page's side; he was given seven years transportation. Curtis, however, was hanged.

32

WOOL IN THE PIE

George Roberts, 11 August 1786

Sheep-stealing has figured prominently in these chronicles so far; we know very little of the actual events surrounding the crimes, but in the case of George Roberts we have an informative account of his end. He was a Lincoln man, and a shoemaker. He was accused of killing and stealing a sheep belonging to a Mr Eastland. He then had the meat baked into a pie – but tale has it that there was still wool on the flesh when the pie was opened, and that is how he was supposedly found out, though it seems a rather tall tale!

Whatever the truth of the discovery and arrest, Roberts found himself facing Mr Justice Willes at the Summer assizes in 1786, and was sentenced to die. The procession in which he walked to the scaffold was documented:

> At about eleven o'clock Roberts was brought out of the city gaol and left in procession up the high street turning around by St Martin's Church. A cart was provided for him, and in it a coffin to receive his body, but Roberts chose to walk.

Roberts prayed and spoke to the crowd, telling them, 'Gentlemen, take warning by me for I dare say there are many present who deserve hanging as much as I do… therefore take warning by my unhappy fate.' As a report at the time expressed it, 'Thus died the man who for a long time had been the terror of the neighbourhood.'

Roberts was executed at the city gaol near Monks Road, where very few hangings took place, and it was 1829 before the gallows were in use again.

Opposite: *The entrance to Lincoln Castle. (Author's collection)*

33

AN APPRENTICE KILLED

William Rawby, 16 March 1787

For centuries, the lot of the English apprentice was miserable as there was little protection from masters who abused them. It was not uncommon at this time to find cruelty against young people in this situation and parish officers were not always vigilant in supervising the placements, and this case from Dogdyke is one of the worst on record.

William Rawby and his wife had a young apprentice: thirteen-year-old Ann Leary. The couple were in the habit of beating the girl, but after going too far, Rawby fetched neighbours to help the suffering girl. Rawby came up with a vague story about how she had become ill. When Ann died, he insisted on preparing her for her coffin, and there is no record of a coroner's inquest. The couple had the girl buried quickly, but they may have done it without following the due process of law, and such a hasty burial called for investigation.

The body was exhumed and the truth of the cruelty to the teenager was soon discovered. The evidence was horrendous: burned feet, a head-wound, and a deep intrusion into the liver. The wounds suggested torture rather than random acts of violence. This was a case of wilful murder. Thirty-seven-year-old Rawby was sentenced to die by Mr Justice Heath on 12 March 1787, and four days later he was hanged, his last words being a plea for his Lord to have mercy on his soul.

34

IN TEARS IN THE CELL

Thomas Dickensen, 23 March 1787

Sheep-stealer Thomas Dickensen was a hardened criminal well known to the local bench, and he did not hold back that fact when he was sentenced to die, and began a lamentable four days of weeping as he waited for the noose.

He had stolen twelve sheep belonging to John Topham of Mablethorpe, but his was hardly an act borne of starvation and desperation. It was a crime committed for profit. Dickenson was from Somercotes, a forty-two-year-old who should have had the wisdom to settle down to an honest life after such a long record of theft. It seems certain that this crime, a capital offence that was not often reprieved, was seen as his worst offence and he was perceived as becoming much more than a petty thief and drunkard.

The lessons had not been learned, and this crime was to be his last. Of course he claimed his innocence: 'I have been guilty of most crimes, except murder, and My Lord, I did not do this one!'

His protestations of innocence were of no use. He walked to the scaffold and the bell rang across the city as the black flag was raised on the instant that his life was extinct.

35

MURDER AT THE TURNPIKE

John Wilson, 14 March 1788

At this time, murderers were unfortunately never hard to find out on the lonesome country of the Fens. They were usually local men and their offences clumsily committed, with witnesses and local reputations well known. With that in mind, it did not take long to catch John Wilson after he had battered to death William Mason, a man from Deeping Fen who was on his way home after a day at Market Deeping. Mason's body was found at the Spalding turnpike in a most appalling condition. His skull was broken and he had multiple fractures to his chin.

The great judge, Lord Eyre, sat in judgement on this brutal killer from Spalding. The accused was not young – he was fifty-four – quite aged at a time when life expectancy

A postcard showing the Pinchbeck road in Spalding. (Author's collection)

was short and work usually crushingly hard. It was a lengthy trial – unusually so for such matters at the time – and it stretched to ten hours. Wilson's pleas and complaints did him no good; he was sentenced to die. However, his sense of injustice remained to the last, when he said, 'I leave behind me a weakly tender wife and I should not wonder if the shock of this will kill her… I suffer innocent as a child… God forbid I should die with a lie in my mouth.'

But he had been proved a vicious killer and a reprieve was not forthcoming. He not only hanged, but his family could not bury his body – his corpse was sent to the surgeons to be dissected.

36

QUADRUPLE NECK-STRETCHING

George Bennett, William Hardy, John Smith & Frances Acred, 20 March 1788

The modern media tends to make Georgian crime acquire something of the supposed glamour of the Dick Turpins and Jack Sheppards – criminals whose exploits figure in literature and film. But there is nothing of that myth about these four lawbreakers. Their crimes were entirely typical of their time and circumstances, as was their hanging.

George Bennett and William Hardy were horse-stealers, and their crimes show the mobility and risky ambition of such thieves and traders, because Bennett took his animal from Yorkshire, and Hardy stole a black colt from a place in Greatford. These were common crimes, and that was the root cause of their capital nature – there had to be a fearsome deterrent.

John Smith was the only violent type in this batch of unfortunates. He viciously attacked and robbed a man named James Dellalah in Boston on the previous December, taking a large sum of money and a bank bill. He had an accomplice named William Nettleship, who escaped on this occasion but was caught and later tried (*see* chapter 37). Frances Acred was tried for stealing steers and heifers from South Somercotes.

All four died together after the 1788 Lent assizes, but we have no clear record of the nature of the execution. It was, even for the hangman, just another execution, as there was no extraordinary drama.

37

OFFENCE UNCERTAIN

George Kilpike, William Nettleship & William Ward, 27 March 1789

Exactly what crime George Kilpike committed is in doubt: he threatened a young woman as she was milking a cow near Waltham and then robbed her of money. The charge was highway robbery (a 'highway' robbery can still be classified as such if it occurs close to a highway), but was it footpad robbery? Whatever the charge, Kilpike was sentenced to die. The accused had an alibi, saying he was in bed at the time of the incident, which the householder confirmed, but she was very old and it seems that the law discounted her statement. In fact, the woman was charged with perjury.

William Nettleship, who had eluded the law at Boston (*see* chapter 36), was now caught and charged – most likely for the same offence for which his accomplice John Smith had died. The condemned man made a speech at the gallows: the usual plea to others to keep on the straight and narrow in life.

As for William Ward, he had been working with a man named Laverick, breaking into property, and they had been charged with a robbery at Leadenham in August the previous year, where they had stolen valuables. The detail that most conveys their nature and attitude is the fact that they had stopped and eaten an apple pie in the process of robbing the house-owner. They were caught within a month (a reward helped in their arrest), and the lucky one was Laverick, who was reprieved and sent to Australia. Ward was hanged alongside Kilpike and Nettleship. We have no information regarding their behaviour in their last moments of life.

38

A HARDENED VILLAIN

John George, 7 August 1789

John George, sentenced to die for burglary and horse-stealing, vehemently told the clergyman who sat with him in the death cell that he was innocent, and said that he knew who was really guilty. It did him no good; he told the crowd that his downfall had been bad company, 'lewd women', and consorting with smugglers.

George had burgled the home of a Mr Stafford at Quadring, for whom he had once worked. He beat the man mercilessly, and then, to make his escape, he stole a mare and rode to Peterborough. As the judge, Mr Justice Grose, said, 'You broke into his house at midnight when he and his family were unsuspecting and asleep and you beat him until he could scarcely crawl.'

When found, George had Mr Stafford's breeches on him, and in the pockets were some papers that clearly incriminated him. The judge could show the man no mercy, saying, 'for mercy to an individual like you would be cruelty to society at large.'

George, also known at times by the name of Smith Flint, had the dubious honour of being reported in the pages of the *Stamford Mercury* – something not usually done at the time. His last desperate pleas to the clergyman were probably his one last throw of the dice, but Lady Luck was long done with him.

39

A LOUTH ROBBERY

John Ward, 19 March 1790

John Ward and John Arsnip robbed a man named Hudson at Louth in January 1790, stealing his spectacles and a silver watch. Lord Baron Eyre, the judge at their trial, was aware that there had been an offer for Arsnip to turn King's evidence and 'shop' his accomplice. The local magistrate had struck a deal with the man, but things were not quite so simple.

Arsnip's evidence was not needed – Hudson had been able to identify both men as his assailants – and both were tried. They were subsequently found guilty and sentenced to hang. Arsnip must have cursed his luck, but he was later reprieved and transported to the colonies; Ward was left to die. Naturally, it was a case of 'thieves fall out' and Ward blamed everything on Arsnip.

In the end, it didn't matter at all. The gallows were waiting for Ward. There is no record of the manner of his death at the rope, but it would be a sure bet that he blamed his absent former friend.

40

STEALING ON WILDMORE FEN

Thomas Rowell, 30 July 1790

This is yet another sheep-stealing case, but this was a large-scale crime. Thomas Rowell stole no less than thirty sheep, the property of William Thacker of Coningsby. Rowell was a farmer from Thornton near Horncastle, and he was apparently in the habit of taking other farmers' animals, as he had also taken six sheep belonging to Josiah Buxton, from Toynton, from Wildmore Fen, the previous Easter.

Extreme poverty was often the cause of this national crime; Rowell, however, was looking for a quick route to wealth and success. All he found was a noose, and his date with destiny was 30 July 1790, after Lord Chief Justice Kenyon uttered the death sentence. It was reported that Rowell wept all the way to the scaffold and had a handkerchief across his eyes so he could not see the seething crowd. He needed the company of a clergyman, Dr Gordon, to the gallows, who prayed with him at every step. Crowds at hangings often did not care for the pitiably afraid: they wanted fortitude and repentance expressed with passion. They were to be disappointed at this one.

41

A MURDER IN THE STABLES

William Burder, 11 March 1791

William Burder was only twenty-seven when he stood trial at a coroner's inquest for the wilful murder of William Harrington. He claimed self-defence, which he maintained at Lincoln when he faced the jury and Mr Justice Grose. They did not accept the self-defence plea. Burder and Harrington had a violent disagreement about a horse in a stable belonging to Anthony Lucas at Spittlegate, Grantham, and Burder claimed that Harrington had started the fight.

Burder was judged to be guilty of murder, as the inquest had originally decided. In fact, when the trial was over and he was in the death cell, Burder confessed that he hated Harrington for turning their employer against him. The clergyman present heard this and must have reported it later. He went to the gallows with great strength of mind, and in his 'last dying speech' he talked about bad company and the folly of his ways.

However, the hanging was seen to be unjust and the crowd staged a riot, damaging the Assembly Rooms. Someone had sawn through the gallows as well, which were needed the next day, so new ones were hastily made. In London, such gallows riots were not uncommon, but in Lincoln this was a rare event.

42

THE DEADLY HORSE TRADE

John Robson, 18 March 1791

The horse-thieving trade covered very wide areas; John Robson and his friend John Davison worked a route between Lincolnshire and Northumberland, and in March 1791 they had stolen four horses from a man named Joseph Pratt in Haltwhistle, and also a mare from a man in Leapwood. They were clearly kept busy taking other men's property. In March their crimes caught up with them and they stood trial for their lives.

The case is a success story for the work of the societies for the prosecution of felons, because the men who were in that society in Northumberland paid for the costs that the amateur sleuths who had followed the robbers south had incurred. At times that tendency for local farmers to join together paid off grandly, and this was one of those times. It also acted as a deterrent to future thieves working the Great North Road and adjoining areas. The two pursuers had stuck to the task, riding a very long way in pursuit of the robbers.

Mr Justice Grose and the jury found both men guilty and they were sentenced to die, but Davison was later reprieved because his argument that he was employed by the victim and was not aware that the horses were stolen was believed. Robson, however, was hanged.

43

A SAD CASE

John Betts & William Campbell, 19 August 1791

William Wright, a farmer of Hagworthingham, was determined to have John Betts, a man in his early twenties, indicted for horse-stealing. The young man had stolen a chestnut horse from the farmer. Baron Hotham at the Summer assizes gave no consideration to the man's youth and the fact that this was his first offence and made sure that the law took its course. Having committed a capital offence, as prescribed by the Murder Acts, Betts was sentenced to die.

William Campbell was a more seasoned and canny criminal. He had come to Lincoln from the Gainsborough Quarter Sessions, where he had been charged with fraud. He had drawn up a bill and dictated a false name for the signature, which he gave as 'Egremont', for the sum of £80. This Winterton man hanged alongside Betts on 19 August 1791.

44

DEATH BLOW
WITH A HAMMER

Ralph Smith, 16 March 1791

Ralph Smith was busy robbing the home of Gentle Sutton of Frampton in February 1791 when the householder came home unexpectedly, only to be dealt a deadly blow with a hammer by Smith. Horrifically, the killer then replaced the hat back on the victim's head to cover a part of the brain which had come out after the fracture.

That report would hardly endear the man to the Lincoln court. Lord Baron Eyre had no mercy in his mind after the villain had been caught, following information given to secure a large reward. The stolen goods had been bought by a tradesman in Fiskerton, and that was enough to sign Smith's death warrant.

This was a heinous crime and a gibbet for the executed body of the killer was erected at the locality of the murder.

45

PERJURY WAS HIS DOWNFALL

John Cocklin, 23 March 1792

Perjury is 'the making of an oath by a witness or interpreter in a judicial proceeding of a statement material in that proceeding which he knows to be false or which he does not believe to be true' (*Osborn's Concise Law Dictionary*). It is a serious affair, and in 1792 it was the downfall of John Cocklin. John and his brother, James, had stolen a ewe from common land at Belton.

James was acquitted but John could not escape his fate at the gallows because he had committed perjury: there had been two false statements by women insisting that the sheep had been bought in Doncaster. When they were shown to be lying, it was all up for the accused.

John Cocklin was hanged, in spite of his repeated pleas of innocence, on 23 March 1792.

46

A SPALDING BURGLARY

John Dinney, 29 August 1794

With rewards offered of more than twenty guineas, it comes as no surprise that burglar John Dinney was tracked down and arrested in October 1793. Lists of the stolen goods had been printed in the local newspapers, including the *Stamford Mercury*, which stated: 'the home of Fairfax Johnson in Spalding had been robbed of linen shirts, silver plate and a diamond ring.'

Dinney had been in gaol in London for robbery, both in Newgate and in the bridewell at Tothill Fields; he was then transferred to Lincoln for the Lent assizes in 1794, but it was not until August that he was finally tried, as there were complications in the preparations for the prosecution. He stood before Lord Baron Macdonald and a long trial resulted in a death sentence.

Everything about Dinney's life seems to have been eventful and complicated, and he was too ill to be hanged immediately after sentencing; even on the day of his execution he had to be helped to walk to the rope, so weak was he. In the more enlightened twentieth century there would have been much more commotion about such a situation, but in 1794 the end was swift and illness was no obstacle to the law taking its course.

47

DESERTER DIES

Edward Coxon, 22 July 1796

Edward Coxon was a deserter from the South Lincolnshire Militia. At this time, Britain was at war with Revolutionary France and there were serious fears of a French invasion. Volunteer regiments were especially valuable, and deserters were dealt with severely. This alone would go against Coxon at trial, but the soldier, along with accomplice William Holmes, had also committed highway robbery.

The two men had attacked William Clarke, a Bourne butcher, who was travelling from the races at Stamford in June 1796. He had tried to run and they shot at him, luckily missing. There was a hue and cry and both attackers were trapped and arrested.

At the Summer assizes, Baron Perryn and his colleagues were in no doubt that this was a capital offence with no complicating circumstances, such as the possibility of manslaughter. The death sentence was passed on both men, with a later reprieve for Holmes. Coxon was hanged as he actually fired the gun.

48

A CLAXBY POISONING

Elizabeth Brocklesby, 17 March 1797

Just seven years before Elizabeth Brocklesby stood in the dock at Lincoln before Lord Baron Macdonald for murder, the punishment of burning at the stake had been abolished. So Elizabeth was spared the flames and was dragged on a hurdle to her fate, to be hanged instead.

She was forty-two years old and was found guilty of poisoning her husband, William, at Claxby near Caistor. Also involved was George Cuthbert, but he was acquitted at trial. Elizabeth was sentenced to hang, and the report states that she was 'taken from the court almost insensible and remained so'. She had to be lifted up from the hurdle to be hanged, and her body was later handed over to the surgeons for dissection. We are not told why Cuthbert was acquitted, however women at this time were supposed to be maternal, caring and protective of life, and thus crimes of homicide were indicative of going 'against nature' and had to be suitably punished, whereas men could be understood in their acts of violence, though not always pardoned of course.

49

CONFESSION AT THE GALLOWS

Thomas Newman, 6 April 1798

Thomas Newman was convicted of highway robbery, in the course of which he robbed, stripped and abused the victim, Jonathan Whiting of Horncastle. He then stole the man's clothes and possessions.

The real sensation here, though, was that Newman, while on the gallows, confessed to an earlier unsolved murder: that of Dr John Bailey at Long Sutton in April 1795.

50

THE 'WHITE LION' ROBBERY

William Jewitt, 21 March 1800

Mr Justice Chambre had something of a reputation for leniency in the courts, and a few years after this particular trial, he was exceptionally merciful to some Luddite rioters in Lancashire. But in the case of William Jewitt, who broke into the White Lion public house in Gainsborough, he showed no pity.

Jewitt and Robinson Middleton stole a silver tankard, a jug, plate and spoons from the pub; Middleton was acquitted but Jewitt was sentenced to hang. He was a Thorne waterman, and tough, but the thought of having his neck stretched was too much; in a faint he had to be roped and pulled up to the platform.

51

A RAPE CASE

William Chapman, 8 August 1800

Cases of rape and sexual assault were not often heard at the assizes at this time. Between 1814 and 1834 there were 166 such convictions in England and Wales, and of these, eighty-one resulted in executions. Although the full circumstances are not clear, it is known that William Chapman sexually assaulted Sarah Rose, a married woman from Roughton, on the road between Dalderby and Horncastle in August 1799.

Part of the problem in unravelling rape cases lies in the blurred definitions as used throughout criminal history. It was not until 1883 that the word 'rapist' was first used, and, as Joanna Burke has written to explain attitudes in the early nineteenth century, 'in the words of the most prominent jurist of the 1830s, it was "almost impossible to rape a resisting woman."'

After a deferral, Chapman was finally tried at the Lent assizes by Mr Justice Brooke and sentenced to die. He was apparently repentant in his last moments.

52

UNDONE BY HIS BREECHES

John Green, 13 March 1801

John Green had been staying at a lodging house run by Robert Lancaster at Kirton, Boston, and, when he left, a watch was found to be missing. Lancaster decided to track him down and challenge him on this, but some time passed before he heard of his whereabouts. When Lancaster did find out where the man was, he set off with Thomas Lunn to find him.

They collared Green in Kirton, at a relative's house, and set off with him to seek a constable. But Green escaped and Lunn went after him. When Lunn did not return there was a search for him, and his body was found in Great Hale Fen. He was almost naked, with no breeches. Green was not very bright: he had returned to his relative's house, where, of course, the constable looked first. He was duly found, in the attic, and brought to justice.

The challenge for the jury was to decide whether this was a case of murder or manslaughter. After all, a man had gone after the accused, and there was no official warrant for the fugitive. But because of the thefts from the body, it was decided that this was a case of wilful murder, and Green hanged.

53

TWO WOMEN TRIED FOR AN EPWORTH MURDER

Susannah Mottershall, 23 July 1801

This is an extremely unusual case: two women tried for murder. Susannah Mottershall stood trial alongside Elizabeth Lamb for the murder of Epworth farmer, Samuel Glew. They were accused of attacking him with an axe, robbing him, and then throwing his body into a ditch.

To makes matters worse, they had stolen property to the very high value of £40. But the common act of turning King's evidence meant that Elizabeth was acquitted and Susannah was left to face the charge of murder alone. When sentenced to die, she made it clear that Lamb was totally to blame and spoke about the dangers of evil influence and bad company. Susannah Mottershall's corpse was dissected, as was the way with executed murderers.

Epworth, showing the crossroads where one killer was buried. (Author's collection)

54

ROBBERS AND FORGER DIE TOGETHER

Matthew Stubley, Edward Taylor & John Whitaker, 31 July 1801

At the Summer assizes, two sheep-stealers and a forger were part of the day's business for the court. Matthew Stubley and Edward Taylor had stolen a few sheep from Castle Bytham, but John Whitaker was altogether a different class of felon. He had been caught in London after forging a receipt for the massive sum of £440 in the name of a Pall Mall firm, Ransom, Morland & Co. It was a daring, high-level crime, and Whitaker was a smooth conman who moved around the country under a number of aliases. But his luck ran out and by means of *habeas corpus* – a legal writ that protects an individual against arbitrary imprisonment by requiring that any person arrested be brought before a court for formal charge – he had been brought to Lincoln from Newgate.

All three men were sentenced to die. Whitaker, being a man of style and dash to the end, arranged for a special coach of mourning to attend him, not the common hanging cart. So it is something of a surprise to learn that Whitaker did not make a dramatic parting speech, given his extravert nature, but he did hold a bunch of flowers in his hand to the very last.

55

TURNED OFF AT NOON

Robert Wells & George Mitchell, 13 August 1802

There is no doubt that in the Regency years there were numerous forgers around, travelling up and down the land, sometimes working in circles of crooks and sometimes alone. Forty-year-old Robert Wells, from Stamford, had uttered (forged) a Bank of England note and had then fled the town to escape arrest. A certain Thomas Rayment of Stamford had found him out and had sworn that there had been a forgery.

Wells was pursued across the country, from Lincolnshire to York, then on to Gretna Green and eventually across the Irish Sea to Dublin. But he was foolish enough to eventually come home: and in the Vale of Belvoir he was spotted and the law informed. He was certainly a slippery customer, being found hiding in a false roof, and he had planned a voyage to France the next day.

In Lincoln Castle he appeared at the same time as horse-stealer George Mitchell, who had stolen a dark bay horse at Boothby Pagnell. Mitchell was pushing his luck, as he had been tried and reprieved from the noose for the same offence a few years before; he was a militia man, and his senior officers had saved his skin on that occasion. He had served a year in prison and then returned to his bad habits.

They died together on the morning of 13 August 1802, Mitchell praying very loudly before being hanged.

56

A BLYBOROUGH MURDER

Thomas Wilson, 14 March 1803

Rabbits were a tempting prey for poachers, and the warren at Blyborough belonging to a Mr Little was defended by two men, including Joseph Lidgett. Just before Christmas 1802, Thomas Wilson decided he wanted a festive feast. But he was seen on Mr Little's land and asked to explain himself, but as he approached the two keepers, Wilson stabbed Lidgett with a sword. The other warrener was armed and he shot Wilson in the arm as he ran off; he made his escape, but he was soon to be found.

The road into Blyborough village. (Author's collection)

Due to his wound, Wilson was forced to consult a surgeon. The surgeon was from Snitterby, just a few miles south, and he had heard of Lidgett's murder, so he told the law that he had been called to see to a gunshot wound. It turned out that Wilson had only just bought the sword he had used, and it had been sharpened just the day before it was used to kill Lidgett. By the end of that fateful week, Wilson was in Lincoln Castle.

The killer was due to suffer in more ways than one; he was sentenced to hang, after he had had his arm amputated. Then, as the judge could not leave Lincoln before the Friday (hanging day), the condemned man had to spend a weekend contemplating his forthcoming death. He was hanged on the Monday, after giving the crowd the familiar words of regret.

57

TOM OTTER GIBBETED

Thomas Temporel, 14 March 1806

Local ghost-hunting groups, most recently the paranormal researchers from Bassetlaw, have spent nights on the premises of the Sun Inn at Saxilby, just outside Lincoln, close to Doddington Hall. Many believe this particular pub to be the most haunted in England. This is surely linked to one of the most brutal and callous murders ever committed in Lincolnshire: the killing by Tom Otter (otherwise known as Thomas Temporel) of his new wife.

Like so many aspects of the Otter story, we are not sure where the truth lies. We can be certain about most of the facts of the murder, although the details about the key witness are troublesome. The witness, John Dunkerly, a casual labourer from north of Drinsey Nook, had enjoyed a night at the Sun in November 1805. Talk must have been full of the Battle of Trafalgar, which had taken place just two weeks before, and other topics related to Napoleon and Nelson. Dunkerly left his friends at around 6 p.m. and started the long walk home across several miles of dark, lonely moorland.

He passed two men he knew near Drinsey Nook, who told him, 'You'll have company, John.' Accounts of Dunkerly suggest that he was a 'peeping Tom' who made a habit of walking out to lonely spots in search of courting couples. Whatever the actual circumstances, he spotted Tom Otter and his wife, Mary Kirkham, together. He later reported that Otter had sat her down and said, 'Sit down, you can rest here.' Otter then walked into the undergrowth and grabbed a hedge-stake. It was 3 November, and the couple had married at South Hykeham only that day; she was pregnant by him and he was forced to marry her. But now, in the darkness, thinking they were alone, he said, 'This will finish my knob-stick wedding' ('shotgun wedding' in modern terms). It certainly did.

Dunkerly noted that:

> The moon shined on his face at the time and his eyes frightened me, there was such a fiery look in them…Then he climbed down to where she was sitting with her head hanging down, and he swung the hedge stake with both hands and hit her a clout on the head. She gave one scream and called on God for mercy, then tumbled over with her head on the ground.

Dunkerly's account is convincing and graphic in its details; he even noted that Mary's body was 'all a-quiver like' before she became rigid. He described the second blow as being like hitting a turnip. With remarkable self-control, Dunkerly kept his silence before apparently passing out. When he awoke, the stake was near him, and there was some of Mary's blood on the sleeve of his smock.

The witness panicked at this and took to wandering around the area for a while, not knowing what to do. But Mary's body was found and Otter was arrested at the Sun Inn, where the inquest was later held. The corpse was taken to the inn after being discovered: blood dripping from the body onto the inn's steps. The hedge stake was also kept at the inn as a piece of customer interest and good local 'spin' for attracting travellers with an interest in gruesome stories.

The trial at Lincoln Castle was of one Thomas Temporel. But whether he was Temporel or Otter is not known. What we know about him is not much: one of the key facts, though, is that he had been married before – to a woman in Southwell. Naturally, Otter would have had to pay for the maintenance of his new wife and child as well as for his existing wife. It is easy to see the problem from his standpoint, but the remedy was the most extreme imaginable.

His trial lasted for five hours, with Justice Graham presiding. Not only was Otter sentenced to hang, but it was also ordered that his body be gibbeted. This was the practice of hanging the corpse of a murderer high above the road as a warning to others to keep to the law. A gibbet was a high post with an arm extended, from which either the entire corpse or a limb would be placed in a cage to waste away and be pecked at by birds. By the end of the eighteenth century, gibbeting was becoming a rare practice; but in the Otter case his deed was so reprehensible that a symbolic token of justice was needed. Otter was hanged on 14 March 1806; the irons and gibbet made for him by Saxilby blacksmith, Dick Naylor. Otter was 'stretched' on Cobb Hall tower at the corner of the castle as the great bell, known as Great Tom, struck twelve.

When the 30ft-high gibbet was raised into position, the weather was severe and there was a strong wind. The beam broke twice, and at one point the metal tackle fell down on the labourers. Dunkerly supposedly said, 'Well, he won't come down no more.' Then Tom Otter's remains fell down on him.

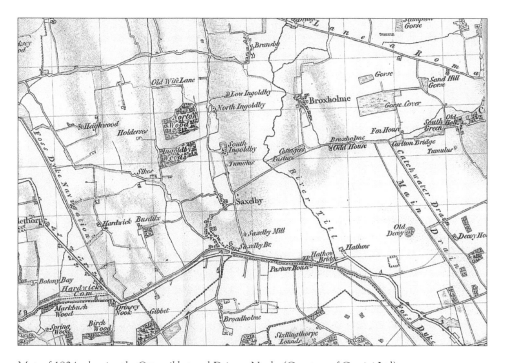

Map of 1824, showing the Otter gibbet and Drinsey Nook. (Courtesy of Cassini Ltd)

The saga of the hedge stake is at the heart of the legend. It was supposed to go missing on 4 November every year; after being fixed to the wall, it still disappeared on the next anniversary. Finally, the Sun landlord sent it to the Peewit Inn not far away. A blacksmith used six clamps to fix it to a wall, but it again went missing. Eventually, by order of the Bishop, the stake was ceremonially burned by the walls of Lincoln Cathedral in early 1807.

John Dunkerly, whether we believe him or not, had undergone far more trauma as a result of witnessing the murder than anyone knew until, as he lay dying, he told the minister who came to his bedside of a terrible haunting, including appearances by the ghost of Tom Otter himself. Dunkerly explained that the worst torments were on the anniversary nights of the murder:

> I felt doley-like so I went to bed about dusk-hours, and what I'm trying to tell you is as true as that I'm a dying man. I couldn't know how sleep and all of a sudden Tom Otter stood in front of me in his chains, and he says, 'It's time. Come along.' And I had to go with him. And he says, 'Fetch it. Make haste.' And I broke into the Sun Inn and fetched the hedge stake from off the nail... when I got outside the door, they were both waiting for me.

The gibbet stayed in place until around 1850. Parts of this terrible object may still be seen by visitors to Doddington Hall. But the myth goes on: the judge, Basil Neild, writes in his memoirs about the case, and recalls a rhyme written as a riddle, composed by an anonymous local poet:

> 10 tongues in one head
> 9 living and one dead.
> One flew forth to fetch some bread
> To feed the living in the dead.

The answer? It's 'The tomtit that built in Tommy Otter's head.'

Doddington Hall, where parts of the gibbet are on display. (Author's collection)

The legend of Tom Otter/Temporel will go on and on, as it has all the elements of a good ghost story, with enough gory elements to keep people awake by the fireside of the Sun Inn.

58

THREE BURGLARS DIE

John Freeman, Charles Metcalfe & Henry Coates, 20 March 1807

These three Brigg labourers decided that they would make some easy money by breaking into a house at Rye Hill, Killingholme, in January of this year. They took a large amount of cash and a gold watch. But another man named Granger informed on them and went free. The whole escapade was partly daring and partly farcical. Charles Metcalfe knew the place as he had worked for the owner at one time, and the gang decided to play around and pretend to be various people in disguise.

They dressed up in all kinds of clothes and even wore false beards; but there the farce ended, because they were armed. Ironically for such a seditious community, Granger made them swear an oath of loyalty. The story later told was that Granger urged them to the deed, even though some were not so enthusiastic when the fantasy turned into reality. When they did enter the house, a fight followed and a shot was fired, but no one was hurt.

After the attack and theft, the news spread across the county and over the Humber, and all were found hiding at various places and arrested. It emerged that they had been responsible for other robberies across that area for some time. Naturally, when all the tales were told in court and it looked as though Granger, who was acquitted, was the leading light of the gang, there were problems. The man seems to have known all the moves and ploys that would get him out of trouble, notably serving in the army, and indeed the last we hear of him is that he was back in the army, on the Isle of Wight.

The scene of the multiple hanging was, of course, very moving: one was a family man, and Metcalfe was emotionally wrecked. The usual final speeches followed and the only concession made by the authorities was that their bodies were not sent for dissection.

59

SILK-EYED JACK HANGS

Charles Wilcock & 'Silk-Eyed Jack', 24 July 1807

Charles Wilcock had once been an upright man, a farmer working in Wragby, but he had fallen into bad ways and lost all respectability. His criminal career was relentless and underhand. He was a specialist in conning and duping people and trying any ruse that might make some easy cash. He tended to buy items in parts and promised to pay when all work was done, but of course never appearing to pay. But one day in Brigg he went too far, forging a bill for the huge sum of £40 and trying to pass it to a publican.

Legend has it that on one occasion he was standing by the gallows in Lincoln when one of his victims said that one day Wilcock would be swinging there. He proved to be right. That was one of the rogues who went to the scaffold: the other was a notable character nicknamed 'Silk-Eyed Jack' from Ludford. He had been practicing his thefts in Birmingham and tended to enjoy stealing horses. But he was caught and sent to Lincoln for trial to answer an earlier charge of stealing a horse at Holbeach the previous May.

From Warwick gaol he came to Lincoln and there he was given the death sentence: he and Wilcock were taken to be strung up, silent and resolute to the end.

60

A MOTLEY CREW HANG

Charles Wakelin, Henry Sawer, William Marshall & John Atkinson,

18 August 1810

Two burglars and two forgers met their doom in 1810 after the court had heard extensive details of their offences. The burglars worked as a gang, and broke into Frow's draper shop in Wrangle in March of this year, stealing a great deal of material worth a massive £300. They had smashed a hole in the wall and rode off with the goods, but they were clumsy.

The robbers were seen on the road with all the fabric and their presence reported by other travellers. They dispersed but the hunt was on, and when they were traced and charged one of the burglars, a man named Allen, turned King's evidence to save his own skin. He made it clear that the others had committed the crime and that he had acted merely as a look-out. Allen's only way out was to join the militia, as so many villains had done before him.

The press took an interest, and the broadside printers told of the gang's reign of terror around Boston, no doubt stretching the truth somewhat. The handbill proclaimed that, 'Large quantities of stolen goods were found in different houses... and concealed in pits...'.

As for Charles Wakelin, the forger, he had been making counterfeit coins, a crime which at that time would guarantee a date with the hangman. The same charge was made against John Atkinson, a young man from Wisbech. He had forged a banker's draft for £100. He had lived under a series of assumed names and clearly worked several frauds, perhaps gaining enough confidence to try such a large sum. He failed, and his attempt to pass the draft in Boston led to suspicion and he was eventually found out when he signed the back of the bill. He later tried to escape and actually managed to get to Minster Yard, where he made a desperate run for his life, reaching Kirton Holme near Boston before he was recaptured.

At the multiple hanging, all the men walked to the scaffold and said a few words; although Atkinson broke down and asked to be lifted up. It was highly irregular, but someone did just that, giving him a moment more of life before he dropped. He was the only felon that day whose corpse was allowed to be taken to his family.

61

FATAL THREESOME

George Rowell & Azubah Fountain, 6 August 1813

At the Fountain's house in Waltham a great deal of drinking was enjoyed, and they were in the habit of making their own elderberry wine. But drunkenness was not the only element in this homicide case. George Rowell and Azubah Fountain, the wife of Robert Fountain, were having an affair, which resulted in the time-old story of 'three is a crowd.'

On 2 July 1813, a surgeon was called to the Fountain house, where he found Robert dead. The account given at the inquest was that Robert had come home very drunk, and that Rowell had sat with him while they drank elderberry wine. Clearly, Rowell thought that it would be assumed that the man had died of drink. But Rowell panicked and changed the story; trying to place the blame on Azubah by recounting a number of times she had sent him to buy laudanum, the standard treatment for almost every illness in that time.

Azubah then changed her story; in court she claimed that the whole idea had been Rowell's, but she could not maintain the performance and cracked under pressure, admitting her guilt. But matters changed again as she came up with another explanation: that she had never given the first statements: no doubt mentioning how much of a home-made brew she had drunk. But that was her death warrant.

Both were found guilty, maintaining different accounts of events to the last. But the basic fact was that Robert Fountain had died of an overdose, and his drunken state was considered to be immaterial in those days of very basic pathology, when assumptions carried more weight than scientific enquiry. They were both hanged and their corpses were soon on the dissecting table.

62

NO DEFENCE

David Spreadbury, 13 August 1813

David Spreadbury travelled the land working forgery scams and living the high-life most of the time, but in Newark, after passing a forged note, he set off by chaise to Grantham, not knowing he was a wanted man. In fact he gave another forged note at Foston toll bar, where he was recognized. There was already a man coming after him from the Kingston's Arms where he had used the first bill.

It was a desperate chase, and, realising too late that he was being cornered, Spreadbury jumped out of the chaise and tried to run for it. But he was caught in Grantham and searched. The rogue had been making a good living – he had £40 cash on him – but he had also tried to hide other forged bills in an alley, which were found.

The man's history was then discovered. He used to be the keeper at a toll bar near Casterton and in that capacity he was robbing the toll commissioners by fraud. He had even tried to set up similar scams in Lincoln. He had left behind him a trail of victims. They were recompensed by the bank – a very honourable gesture on their part. As for the condemned man, he spoke of his moral ruin as he stood by the noose, just what the crowd expected.

63

LAST HANGING ON

BURTON ROAD

William Ward, 1 April 1814

Many people driving past the small roundabout that leads onto Burton Road today would never think it was the place where hangings were carried out, but so it was, until William Ward was hanged there on April Fools' Day, 1814.

These were hard times, and robbery was common. Ward and his friend Bell were labourers from Retford, but in March of this year they were up to no good in the village of Mareham-le-Fen: they burgled a draper's shop and stole cloth and cord worth around £200. They were caught after stealing a boat belonging to Mr North, a farmer from Revesby; he saw them as he was on Wildmore Fen, and was observant enough to notice that the boat was stacked with goods – the stolen fabric.

The robbers were approached, and claimed that they had simply found the farmer's boat, but Mr North went for help and soon the two robbers were in custody. In fact, the citizens who made the arrest were lucky not to have been maimed or even killed, because in doing so Ward tried to shoot them, but the gun did not function. However the intent was there and that action was his death warrant. The fact that Bell did not have a gun saved his neck. In court at Lincoln, their defence was that they had been paid to try to recover the goods, but it was an easy matter to discredit that tale and they were sentenced to die. The hangman was a convict who acted as the executioner to have his sentence commuted.

64

TWO BANKERS HANG

Thomas Clarke & Henry Coster, 28 July 1815

In Lincolnshire, the term 'bankers' does not imply cashiers or employees of savings banks, but men who carried out the tough, demanding work of navvying on the many waterways. It was small pay for hard labour, and it was tempting for some to make quick money illegally. So it was with Thomas Clarke and Henry Coster, who robbed a draper's shop of a massive amount of stock worth £400. But the draper, Elderkin, had them in his sights and he brought a constable to Clarke's home in Pode Hole; there they found the stolen goods along with the tools of the man's nefarious trade of burglary – including a gun.

Thomas's son, John, was sent to warn Coster that his place was about to be searched too, but he was later removed from the list of arraignments. There was no real defence and the result was a death sentence for both men.

What is particularly interesting in this case is its contribution to our understanding of social history with regard to the nature of authority and lawlessness at this time. The large number of fellow bankers around the area were supposedly planning to act against the forces of law to stop the hangings; there were some men seen on the south wall of the castle on the day before the execution, but they were fired at and, of course, the watch then had notice and so strengthened all security measures. The most effective of these preventative measures was to have the hangings inside the walls rather than on the walls in the tower; it worked, and both men died without incident, except that Coster gave an entertaining last speech before throwing his shoes into the crowd.

Their bodies were not sent for dissection, but to their banker friends.

65

ANTIMONY KILLS A CHILD

Elizabeth Whiting, 15 March 1817

In the nineteenth century there were so many domestic uses for poisons that accidents, as well as intended poisonings, were frequent. Add to that the extreme poverty and deprivation among the lowest labouring class and you have a certain number of explanations for wrongdoing. Infanticide was common among women from the working class and, in spite of supervision, it was often in workhouses that such crimes occurred. Such was the case with Elizabeth Whiting, who was living in Kirton workhouse when she committed this crime.

Elizabeth already had two children, but was a pauper when she gave birth to a third child in July 1816. Elizabeth applied butter of antimony to her baby's food, and also used Bateman's drops (something she herself had taken previously): the child died in agony. It seems that Elizabeth had been told by the mistress of the workhouse that the antimony, used for dressing lambs' feet, was very poisonous. Thus all the court in 1817 could see she was intent to kill the child.

The child's horrible death was described with no compassion: at the first hearing, in the coroner's court in Boston, the facts about the poison were given and statements made by medical men. Elizabeth Whiting had the distinction of being the first person hanged at Cobb Hall, at which event the crowd would have heard the condemned woman shout out to her Lord for mercy.

66

A SURFLEET MURDER

Elizabeth Warriner, 26 July 1817

This case is far more complex than the two basic facts of the killing imply: these are first, that eleven-year-old John Warriner was found hanging and near death, and second, that on being put to bed he was sick and in agony, having been poisoned.

The finger of blame pointed at Elizabeth Warriner, his stepmother and second wife of Surfleet man, Joseph Warriner. Joseph came home to find his son dead, and his first words were: 'Damn your eyes, you've done it at last!' Earlier in that day, a witness named Alice Styles had been at the house when the boy was dying and she referred to the boy being sick and bringing up something 'with an offensive smell.' Elizabeth would not have a doctor brought and in conversation she had said, 'For heaven's sake say nothing Alice, or you will hang me.'

We know nothing about the personal circumstances or state of mind of the accused; only that her enmity towards the boy was well known. Of course, she was arrested and charged and the coroner stated that there was a charge of wilful murder against her. At Lincoln the reasons for the boy supposedly hanging himself were not apparent, and so it was thought that the hanging had been Elizabeth's first strategy, before the poison being used. The trial lasted five hours, but a guilty verdict was returned.

It is hard to imagine the pathetic sight of the woman in the courtroom, then delivered of her third child and suckling him as she sat in the dock. The child was taken from her and she was duly hanged.

67

BAD CHARACTER MEETS HIS END

William Longland, 15 August 1817

This is an unusual case, although the burglary to which it relates is very ordinary. A gang of men were involved in robbing the premises of Sarah Morgan in Grantham in April 1817, but William Longland was the only member hanged because his charge was 'counselling, aiding and being accessory to the robbery'. A report at the time states that he gathered and primed the gang, who met at the Lord Nelson pub in Gonerby Hill Foot to plan the burglary. It was reported that Longland organised the crime and that he expected a good share of the profits. They took bedclothes, sheets and blankets – and for such trivial items, Longland was hanged.

At the heart of his trail was the fact that he was a known 'bad character' in the Grantham area, and was the 'puppet master' of previous similar gangs. The judge, as he put on the black cap, talked about 'cold-blooded but miscalculated villainy' of such men who 'avoided danger themselves but incited others to commit crimes and corrupt the morals of younger men.' It seems he had finally been caught because an informer in the gang reported their intention to rob Miss Morgan's home.

68

A MULTIPLE HANGING

Richard Randall, John Tubbs, Thomas Evison & Thomas Norris,
27 March 1818

Richard Randall and John Tubbs were labourers out for some villainy in March 1818. Tempted by the sight of a rich man, William Rowbotham of Holbeach, and his servant on the road, the two men dragged him from his horse and attacked him before making off with a silver watch and some money.

But they did not bargain for the alertness and quick thinking of a Whittlesey constable, who responded to information about the watch being sold, and went to investigate. He had heard of the robbery and checked the facts of stolen items, then went looking for the men.

It was a remarkable chase – the constable tracked them down through Lincolnshire and into Norfolk, finally cornering them at Cromer. The full story came out in the confession, where it transpired that there had been a third man involved, and that Tubbs had not actually been directly involved, but merely in reserve. That did not stop Tubbs from being a prominent member of the gang, and he too was arrested soon after. It was Tubbs who was to be considered thoroughly nasty and culpable, as he had once been employed by Mr Rowbotham – a betrayal that was always severely dealt with – so both men were to hang.

Thomas Evison and Thomas Norris were arsonists: they had burned an oats hovel and threshing machine belonging to Mr Faulkner at Anwick in January. The usual action of advertising a reward had brought them to justice; in addition, there was a witness who had heard Evison threaten to do the burning, and Evison's stupidity in asking about turning King's evidence is almost too crass to be believed. A large crowd watched all four men die at Cobb Hall. No particularly striking last speeches were made.

69

A VIOLENT BURGLARY

John Louth, 19 March 1819

This sad tale could be called 'Hanged for a Tea Caddy' because that, along with a few other items, was what John Louth was executed for in March 1819. Along with his accomplice, a young man named Parker, Louth broke into the home of Mr Plowright at Pinchbeck. The two burglars were in their twenties, labourers from Spalding. They were violent and were likely to raise hell when annoyed, and that is what happened one fateful night in Pinchbeck in November 1818.

They were looking for somewhere to stay – at least that is the story they told Mr Plowright, but when refused entry they smashed in the door, putting a gun-barrel through the hole and terrifying the residents. The rogues broke in and found that they had the ground floor to themselves – the Plowright family had gone upstairs and shut themselves in one of the bedrooms. After a fearful night, the family ventured forth to find that objects were missing from the house. A constable was soon on the thieves' trail. Later, following their arrest, the full details of what they had done came out in court. One witness described how she had been assaulted and threatened by Louth, a sorry tale that probably swung everything against him. There was nothing either could say to defend what they had done, but clearly Louth was the more offensive and violent, and he was sentenced to hang while Parker was reprieved.

ONE HUNDRED POUNDS REWARD.

The Committee of the GRIMSBY ASSOCIATION for the Prevention and Detection of Incendiarism, offer a Reward of ONE HUNDRED POUNDS for the Discovery of the Person or Persons who maliciously set on fire the CORN-STACKS, &c., of MR. RICHARD FAULDING, of Waltham, on Wednesday Evening the 26th of November last, to be paid on conviction of the Offender or Offenders.

BY ORDER OF THE COMMITTEE.

Great Grimsby, Dec. 9, 1834.

Notice issued by the Society for the Prevention of Incendiarism. Such societies were against all rural crime, including animal stealing and maiming. (Skelton Collection, Grimsby)

70

HANGED FOR HORSE-STEALING

Richard Johnson, 6 August 1819

In the year 1819, remembered for the Peterloo Massacre in Manchester, the only hanging in Lincoln was that of a horse-stealer. Richard Johnson had stolen three horses and was making a tidy profit from that business. He would travel to distant places, even as far as Helpston in Northamptonshire, then he would steal a horse and ride it home to South Kyme.

Johnson carried out at least three of these thefts: at Croxton Kerrial where he stole two horses, and one at Helpston, but he may have stolen many more. The profit was grand indeed – he sold the horse from Helpston for 25s. But he was soon noticed, questioned and then arrested. It was a time when this particular offence was very common and the judge at Lincoln wanted to make an example of Johnson; he was only twenty, but there was no mercy with regard to his youth. The fact that there had not simply been one theft was the aspect of the case that the judge saw as warranting the death penalty.

71

A MERCILESS RAPE

William Fox, 17 March 1820

William Fox was just twenty-one years old when he approached a married woman, Mary Rhodes, as she was milking cows at Tathwell. She was only half a mile from home, but nobody heard her cries for help as Fox attacked and then raped her. She was at his mercy for half an hour before they were disturbed by the woman's husband, William, who grabbed the attacker.

The rapist offered money for the offence to be left without recourse to the law, but then escaped whilst William helped his wife. The rapist then apparently told the landlord of a nearby pub the events of the day. That was surely an act of suicidal nature; he must have known the consequences of arrest and trial. However, not all rape charges at the time led to the gallows, so maybe he was concocting a story to partly blame the poor victim.

Whatever the truth may be, he faced the judge and jury in Lincoln and just two days later was hung.

72

A ROBBERY PLANNED IN MANCHESTER

David Booth & John Parrish, 23 March 1821

With this story, we have a witness to events who was then a famous radical activist and is now one of the most celebrated Lancashire working-class heroes from those tough days of the struggle for rights for ordinary people: Samuel Bamford. Bamford was a prisoner in Lincoln Castle in 1820, sentenced for his part in the Peterloo Massacre, Manchester, when ordinary people had been cut down and killed by hussars while attending a meeting. In his classic book, *Passages in the Life of a Radical*, he recalls life in Lincoln Prison at this time, and also tells the tale of two men, David Booth and John Parrish. Bamford must have been a bitter man as he came into the gaol, and he was to see many other gaols in his tempestuous life.

Mr Justice Richardson had led the trial of these two men, who had burgled the house of an old woman in Whaplode. Parrish had been a shepherd to Mrs Cully and wrote to the men he had met in Lancashire. Bamford explains why that connection was there: 'It was a custom... for harvest men to go from Lancashire to Lincolnshire – a "cwokin" as they called it – and a party of these from Astley Bridge had been in the habit of doing the harvest work...'. Bamford notes that the robbers went to the farm dressed as mummers, and then, 'The robbers next tied the inmates fast and plundered the house of about £900 worth of plate, money and notes...'.

Although they had been masked, Booth's mask had fallen off and he was seen, and so he was soon tracked down. Bamford wrote that, 'The hounds of the law soon laid on the true scent and set off for Lancashire with the speed but not the noise of bloodhounds.' Some of the robbers had fled overseas, but in the end Parrish and Booth were in court and sentenced to hang.

The events leading to their deaths were witnessed by Bamford, who described the scene:

> It was rather a cloudy and gusty morning when, getting up to my window, I beheld the gallows fixed, and two halters ready noosed, swinging in the wind. To me, this first sight of the instrument of death was both melancholy and awful. I placed myself on the rampart leading to the tower, on which stood the gallows, and had a full view of the criminals as they crossed the green. First came the Governor, bearing a white wand; then some halberdiers and other sheriff's men, then the deputy sheriff, next came the criminal, then the chaplain, the turnkey, the executioner and assistant and other javelin men...

The Lancashire man also saw the two felons die: 'The shepherd appeared to have his eyes fixed on the instrument of death from the moment he came in view of it', and, 'he appeared faint and required assistance to mount the ascent.' Booth, wearing a blue coat, was 'more dogged in his manner', and 'he held his head a little on one side, gave a glance at the gallows, spat out some white froth... and went on again without help.'

The bodies were removed 'on the backs of men' after they had been left hanging there for an hour. They were laid side by side on the floor of the Town Hall.

A portrait of Samuel Bamford, from his memorial stone. (Author's collection)

73

WIFE MURDER AT WHAPLODE

James Cawthorne, 9 August 1821

This heartless killing at Whaplode had the dubious distinction of making the national news – at least it was reported in *The Annual* register for this year. That report had a few details wrong, such as the killer's age and the name of the victim, but it did say that the murderer behaved 'in a hardened manner' and that sums up this brutal man.

James Cawthorne was a labourer who had taken his wife's life first by giving her arsenic mixed with thickened milk, and then, after seeing her suffer for four days, strangling her. That meant that there were two charges, and after some debate it was decided that both prosecutions would go ahead and then the judge, Mr Justice Park, directed that he would put the charge to the jury when proceedings had run their course.

There was evidence from a neighbour, who said that Cawthorne had come home feeling ill, had been given the warm milk, and then sent his wife, Mary, for some beer. On her return, she finished off the milk and was afterwards violently ill. This evidence, however, was deemed inadmissible because it was allegedly based upon hearsay put together after the event, largely because of a love letter written by the killer to a woman in the village stating that he should 'go through a dismal death' and 'for the love' of her.

There was evidence of a death by poisoning, but no definite identification of any substance, but the jury were sure that Cawthorne was guilty of wilful murder and he was hanged.

74

HIGHWAY ROBBERY ON MARKET DAY

John Rogers, 22 March 1822

This was a case of robbery on the highroad, and there were four men involved in the assault on Christopher Craven, from whom a large sum of money and a silver watch were stolen. In addition to John Rogers, John Edgoose and his son William, were part of the gang. There was also another man, John Jackson, who later turned King's evidence and told the tale, claiming that he was talked into joining them.

With the exception of John Edgoose, who had been involved in directing and advising the nature of the robbery, the gang left to do the robbery, having been given guns by the older man. As it turned out, Rogers actually did the deed; the others were too afraid and hid. The robbers were arrested at Swineshead and it became clear that the Edgoose family were a criminal gang who had narrowly escaped punishment previously. But their luck held out again, Rogers taking the brunt of the prosecution and going to the scaffold. It transpired that he had committed a similar robbery at Donington the previous year.

75

ROBBERY AND ASSAULT AT CAISTOR

Joseph Burkitt, 2 August 1822

Joseph Burkitt and fellow thug George Barton conducted a reign of terror around the village of Caistor in the years before their robbery of John Twigg in July 1822. That was the end of the road for them; after attacking and robbing Twigg, with some support from a certain William Goodwin, the terror was to end in transportation for life for Barton and Goodwin, and death for Burkitt.

Twigg was travelling to Market Rasen after a day in Hull when he was confronted by the gang. Burkitt hit him, and then he was robbed of cash, his watch, and even his overcoat. But Burkitt's effrontery was matched by his stupidity, for he later walked boldly around the fair at Caistor, and of course Twigg, looking out for him, identified him and had him arrested.

On the scaffold, Burkitt, who was married with children, simply said, 'farewell'. The crowd were robbed too – of the satisfaction for a speech of repentance and some expected tremours of abject fear.

76

'THE COMMISSION OF UNNATURAL CRIMES'

William Arden, Benjamin Chandler & John Doughty, 21 March 1823

Death and persecution was usually the fate of the sodomite at this time, and historians have demonstrated that in the early years of the nineteenth century more men were either executed or imprisoned for the crime than in any other period in the history of England. Various types of bestiality are in the chronicles of crime, and in Victorian England there were rare cases of sexual intercourse with animals, a crime which usually resulted in death, as in the case of an old man hanged at Ilchester for 'bestiality with a cow'. In fact, as late as 1883 at Lincoln, there was a case of such bestiality, and it involved a young man named Miller who was given ten years penal servitude for bestiality with a ewe. But sodomy was, although equally problematical in court in some ways, more clear-cut in the early decades of the nineteenth century. In this case, the three accused had allegedly had 'a beastly and unnatural connection' with the body of Henry Hackett, a draper's apprentice. The problem was that Hackett, only nineteen, had turned King's evidence against the three men, although he may have consented, and indeed it looks as though he did.

Reports on such things were reported in a coy and bland way, and one such account of this case was focused on the phrase, 'the commission of an unnatural crime.' Before Mr Justice Park in the September assizes, the three were found guilty of the crime and, of course, there was scandal and revulsion in the newspapers. Arden and Chandler were from London, where Chandler had been a valet to the Duke of Newcastle; Doughty was a Grantham man. One contemporary broadside ballad imagines an account of the case written by the judge, and has verses such as these about Arden:

> He laid his plans both deep and strong
> His wickedness to hide
> And thought his foul and secret ways
> In safety would abide.

> He was the head of all the gang
> In London did he dwell;
> A fair and proper house he kept
> In Pulteney Street as well.

When Lord Denman proposed changes in the criminal law in correspondence in 1837, he proposed to reduce the number of capital crimes, but kept sodomy, along with murder and treason, as hanging offences. Between 1839 and 1848 there were 640 capital sentences in England, these included murder, malicious wounding, burglary, rape, robbery, arson, riot, returning from transportation, High Treason, and sodomy. Clearly, the offence was still rated very highly on the scale of infamy, and strangely, in the ecclesiastical courts, there were cases of marital disputes which had in them instances of sodomy as important elements in the appellants' causes of litigation.

77

ARSENIC IN ALFORD

John Smith, 15 March 1824

John Smith went to buy a pound of arsenic from a druggist in Alford just a few days before Jane Arrowsmith had to send for a doctor after eating some cake. Jane was pregnant, and suffered a miscarriage during the worst period of torment in the throes of the poisoning. Following her death, the pathologist found that there was arsenic in her body.

Suspicion turned on Smith, the father of her child and would-be father of the child who had been miscarried. Before she died, Jane told officials that John had made the cake and told her that it was just for her, and that no one else should eat it. They were due to be married very soon as the banns had been proclaimed. This was more than a case of cold feet – it was vicious, brutal murder, carefully planed and with terrible results.

John Smith was found guilty and he was hanged before a seething crowd at Cobb Hall.

78

THROAT CUT TO ESCAPE THE NOOSE

James Wetherill, 20 August 1824

When James Wetherill was locked up at Brigg on suspicion of the murder of William Burridge, he tried to defeat the process of law by slashing his throat. But he did not die; a surgeon was sent for and Wetherill told the surgeon all the details of the murder and robbery he had committed.

He had been a sailor and had travelled far north, but his original trade was that of a chimneysweep. He was in his early twenties, and decided that the quickest way to get some money would be to rob someone. He had a gun, and he waited on the Wrawby road for father and family man Berridge to come along the road, and there he shot him dead before helping himself to the contents of his victim's pockets. It was a ruthless and cowardly crime, committed in the dead of night.

Statements were made saying that Wetherill had been seen digging at his father's house just after this killing. The constable found gunpowder on his clothes and a pistol he had tried to bury. Then the confession was made after his life had been saved. All that injury achieved was a stay of execution; he was found guilty but, of course, his throat would have to heal before he could be hanged. Chief Justice Beal passed the death sentence, and it was twelve days before the man was fit to hang. Wetherill's body was later dissected by the surgeons.

79

'WHAT'S HANGING? I CARE NOTHING FOR IT!'

William Udale, 23 March 1827

Richard Peel of Long Sutton found he was short of eight of the sheep in his flock in December 1826. His shepherd reported the theft and there was a search; it took only until the next day for information to be gained, as some of the animals were discovered on Mr Richardson's farm at Chatteris, and the story given was that William Udale had brought them. Sheep-stealers always had the problem of where to keep their booty, and it was a dangerous habit to lodge them in temporary quarters. Udale had painted over the sheep, so that the colours showing they belonged to Mr Peel were not visible.

It was often the case with rural crime at this time that the criminals knew or had worked for their victims, and Udale had indeed once been employed by Peel. He was found guilty in Lincoln, and it was clearly theft for profit rather than for necessity; the latter circumstance would have meant transportation. But the noose was waiting for Udale, and the pathetic sight of his family coming to see him before he died was one of the saddest things the prison staff had to witness.

Udale addressed the spectators, saying, 'What's hanging? I care nothing for it!' After hanging, the thief's body was buried at St Nicholas's Church, and it is on record that a massive crowd attended.

80

ROBBERY AT CROSS O'CLIFF HILL

George Wingfield, 27 March 1829

This was not a propitious year for thieves. Sir Robert Peel's Police Act had been passed and the first fully professional police force was on the streets of London. But in Lincolnshire it was to be another twenty years before anything similar was to come into being. None of this was in the thoughts of George Wingfield as he lay in wait for a victim on the road towards Sleaford. Two men came along, and he sprang out and struck one, a Mr Fountain, on the head; the horse ran off, leaving a Mr Robert Capp next in line to be attacked. He was beaten up and robbed of the large sum of £23.

There seemed to be no need for a police force, because back in Lincoln someone reported seeing Wingfield up in that area, close to a toll-bar. It was merely a matter of finding him, and that was soon accomplished. He had the victim's pocketbook on him when found. It was a sad case of a fall from respectability into roguery, because the robber had been a person well known and regarded in Lincoln, but he had become depraved, in spite of having a family.

From the Flying Horse tavern where he was found, Wingfield next found himself standing in the dock at Lincoln before Mr Justice Burrough. The accused tried to blame an accomplice, but to no avail. The accomplice was transported but Wingfield was hanged. His death was intended to act as a deterrent to locals because he was from the city.

81

ROUGH TOM DIES

Timothy Brammer, Thomas Strong & John Clarke, 19 March 1830

Timothy Brammer was a banker, that rough breed of navvies who often lived outside the law. A Worksop man, he was an exceptionally tough character, tall and strongly built, and known by several other names locally, including Tiger and Rough Tom. He led a gang of burglars and knew no fear, but he was collared after a job done at Hawstead Hall and he was to be tested in court.

A witness to the crime spoke against them, naming Brammer, who stood stone-faced throughout. The other rogue, Thomas Strong, had left the county, going as far as London to try to escape notice, but the forces of law found him. By this time there was a rudimentary system of advertising rewards and describing wanted men across the country, notably in London, and that was the least dangerous place for a fugitive to run to. Both men were arrested and brought to Lincoln.

All the men could do was say that the witness, a Mr Elsey, had lied, but nothing would persuade the jury that there was any other verdict than guilty. The gang of bankers indulging in the burglaries was extensive and some others got away without being traced. It was to be a triple hanging, as John Clarke was sentenced to die for stealing two sheep at Freiston in January of that year: he was actually seen driving the sheep home and soon traced. He had no explanation and was found guilty.

The tough banker and his mate were, of course, an attraction for the locals, who liked 'a good hanging' better than most entertainments. On top of that, three men were to die, so it was particularly inviting. The newspaper reports stressed that the criminals 'walked steadily to the drop' and that Brammer was 'unflinching but had lost much weight.' He had the order of hangings change so that he could die beside Strong, and again, as other bankers had done, they threw their boots to the crowd. The big Worksop man fought hard against the rope, the report saying that 'his legs were nearly drawn up to his chest before slowly relaxing again.' His father was allowed to take the son's body away, rather than there being any transfer to the surgeons.

82

KILLER IN THE BARN

Michael Lundy, 12 March 1831

On a farm near Lincoln, Thomas Sewards and his son-in-law, Michael Lundy, were doing some seasonal work for the farmer. They were heaping and burning weeds in the July of 1851, and, after they had eaten their evening meal, the farmer offered them his barn for the night, as they were due to start work again early the next morning. The farmer, Wilson, saw that Sewards was not well, and he put out some straw and sacks for the two Irishmen, also giving them a key so they could secure themselves for the night inside, if they wished.

Sewards could not speak English, but he was not well, and Wilson negotiated with Lundy. As time went on and evening came, the two men were in the barn, but then around eight, Lundy was seen sitting outside by a carpenter's bench, surrounded by the man's tools. This was a long way from the Wilsons' farmhouse, and all seemed well, but an hour later, as Mrs Wilson was feeding poultry, she heard a cry of murder and saw Lundy, only half-dressed, acting crazed and ranting.

The man then told a long and far-fetched account of being accosted by 'a tall black man, six feet high with a broad-brimmed hat' who asked Lundy if he wanted some company, and had supposedly insisted that he sleep with the labourer. Lundy even claimed that he had had a fight and been pelted with stones. Mrs Wilson did see that there was a swelling on his forehead, seeming to confirm the story. But when the Wilsons went to investigate the situation at the barn, they were understandably shocked at the horrendous sight that met their eyes when they walked inside.

There was Sewards, with a carpenter's axe buried in his face, cutting him down to the mouth; there was also a wound on his scalp. Lundy all this time was screaming and muttering a prayer, not daring to go near the body.

The Wilsons naturally set no credence on the tale of the tall black man and they carried Lundy off to a constable at Elthorpe; the body was then taken there on a cart. It soon became apparent that Lundy had been in a fight; there was blood sprinkled on his trousers and coat. He later washed his hands – in contrast to their very dirty state as observed earlier by the Wilsons. On investigation, the constable found the imprint of a naked foot by a pond close by, and when the man was searched, 6s were found on him. The Wilsons said that when they had first met the Irishmen, they had seemed quiet and peaceable.

Lundy, after this murderous rage, became yet another client for the hangman at Cobb Hall, Lincoln Castle.

83

BURGLARY OF A FATHER-IN-LAW

John Greenwood, 18 March 1831

This is possibly the only capital crime in the nineteenth century recorded as taking place at Theddlethorpe All Saints. John Greenwood was a sailor, but he turned his hand to crime and he burgled the home of an old man, John Weatherhogg. He was not subtle: he scrambled his way in via a plank of wood to a window, and, once inside, fired shots at the elderly man.

After that Greenwood struck the victim with a poker and proceeded to rob him of anything of any value, including a knife, a spoon and some cash. But unfortunately for the attacker, Weatherhogg recognised Greenwood's voice.

Greenwood was soon caught, being apprehended by a constable near Tetney. In court, Baron Vaughan passed the death sentence, and the man's claim that it was only his first offence did no good at all. Desperately, the condemned man tried to run away across the yard at the castle, but he was destined for the noose. Once again, the case proved the speed and efficiency of the village constables, even in the years before any professional forces existed.

84

A FATAL FIGHT IN GRIMSBY

William Hall, 22 July 1831

William Hall liked a drink. In fact he liked to have an enormous quantity of drink, and that always led him into trouble. In July 1831 it led him to the gallows in Lincoln.

Hall, just twenty-two, was out filling himself with beer one June evening in Grimsby when he made too much noise for Edward Button, who lived near the local alehouses. Hall was making a nuisance of himself in a pub run by a Mr Kempsley and Button came to help the landlord throw the drunkard out into the street. After Hall was turfed out, Button still kept on his case, shouting through a window, 'Take him to the gaol, the rascal deserves to go for making such a row on a Sunday night.' Button was being a good citizen, expressing his moral views openly. The problem was that Hall felt that deeply and he vowed revenge.

'I'll kill Kempsley and somebody else!' he roared as he sharpened a knife on a stone a few days later. A witness heard him make that awful oath. A man named Milner, who spent time with Hall, monitored the progress of the man's rankling hatred of the landlord and of Button.

Nothing much happened for a few days, but on 2 July, Milner went out drinking with a man named Joseph Nash and also with Edward Button. They went along to the Duke of York, run by a Mrs Dines, and much later on, near midnight, Hall and his friend Ratton came in; Hall was out to provoke Button and he succeeded. According to a witness, their conversation went as follows: Button said, 'Hello! What do you want?'

'One bully has as much right here as another,' Hall answered, and Button followed that with a blow to Hall's face. Milner said that at first Button never even moved from his chair, but soon after there was a direct confrontation. Hall strode across to the far corner of the inn and challenged his enemy. 'I'm ready for you any time!'

A Lincoln pamphlet on the event reports the fight as being a desperate affair: 'In a short time both parties fell to the floor; they fell in the doorway leading from one room into another, there was no light in the other room, but it was not very dark where they fell…'. What happened next must be a familiar tale from many a drunken brawl: one of the men had a knife and, of course, it was Hall. From the struggle on the floor Button emerged,

Trial and Execution of William Hall, for the
MURDER OF EDWARD BUTTON,
AT GRIMSBY. Executed at Lincoln, July 22, 1831.

WILLIAM HALL, a young man, scarcely attained the age 22 years, when he was convicted for the wilful murder of Edward Button, under the following circumstances: it was clearly proved on the trial that Hall was intoxicated on the Sunday, (a week previous to the murder being committed) and that Button had assisted in putting him out of a public house kept by Mr. Kempsley, where he was making a disturbance, after he was turned out Button said through the window, "take him to the goal, the rascal deserves to go for making such a row on a Sunday night," from this it appears that Hall took offence, and vowed he would have revenge if it was seven years first; one witness swore to having seen him on the Wednesday sharpening a knife on a stone, and again on Thursday he see him sharpening the same knife on a stone trough in Mrs. Dines' yard. it was a small pointed shut knife, with a bone haft, he sharpened the point of it. When he had done his knife he swore he would kill Kempsley and somebody else, but he did not say who: he said "I'll kill Kempsley and somebody else." it was about dusk. the knife might be four inches altogether; from this time to the night of the murder nothing particular appears to have occurred. The awful murder took place at the Duke of York public house, in Grimsby, on Saturday night, July 2nd, 1831 Wm. Milner, one of the principal witnesses gave evidence to the following effect; he stated that himself, Edward Button, & Joseph Nash, went to Mrs. Dines', the Duke of York Inn, between 11 and 12 o'clock at night: William Hall came in about half an hour afterwards

A broadsheet account on the trial and execution of Edward Button. (Ref. HILL 41/5/26. With the permission of Lincolnshire Archives)

staggering into the light for all to see; then he managed to walk to a chair and sit down, clearly in great pain and bleeding. Someone at the scene said that he ground his teeth together and then died instantly.

A man opened Button's waistcoat because the crowd thought he was having a fit, but then he saw 'a wound on the fellow's breast.' The landlady screamed out loud that a man had been stabbed. As for Hall, he still had the wit to try to throw away the weapon; he appears to have gone outside to do that and then go back inside the inn where someone shouted, 'Hall, you have stabbed this man with a knife.' Hall said he had no knife on him.

Naturally, everyone knew that he had been outside to throw away the murder weapon. Later in court, the daughter of the landlady said that she heard Hall provoke Button, saying, 'Come on!' She said he had one arm behind him – that was where he held the knife. She said that she followed the fight, holding a candle, and she said that she saw Hall holding Button fast to the ground, with a knee on him, and then the killer knocked away her candle. Before the light was out, though, she said, 'I saw a knife in Hall's hand.' She was not the only one present who saw it.

Evidence from the local surgeon confirmed that Button had suffered a deep two-inch long wound by his sternum and the knife 'had passed through the integuments in an oblique direction, upwards and inwards, entering between the fifth and sixth ribs.' The doctor stated that there was no doubt that the knife-wound had caused the death of the deceased. In court, all this was heard in silence by the man in the dock, and he had nothing to say before a guilty verdict was passed on him.

The judge donned the black cap and sentenced Hall to hang, at which point the court reporter noted that, 'The prisoner, during the whole of the trial, preserved a remarkable indifference to his fate, but afterwards he manifested a very different spirit.' The judge commented on 'the premeditated malice in the prisoner's mind, in having, on two separate occasions, sharpened a knife with a cool and deliberate intent to use such a weapon against one, if not two persons…'.

The reporter went on, saying that Hall's behaviour was then 'truly becoming, neither displaying excess of timidity not unbecoming confidence, but looked forward to his approaching fate with calmness and resignation.' The assembled crowd by the tower at Cobb Hall, Lincoln Castle, had what they thought was good entertainment, many paying for the best views of the hanging from the inns across the road. They even enjoyed a long sermon on the sins of the condemned man. Hall must have wished he could have had more than the traditional final drink of ale at The Struggler public house by the castle walls.

85

ARSON AT LUSBY

Richard Cooling & Thomas Motley, 29 July 1831

The early 1830s were years in which there were widespread rural troubles called 'Captain Swing' – agrarian riots and damage to property stemming from the poverty of labourers. As one local constable wrote in his journal: 'About this time there was a great deal of burning and plundering about the country. They burnt Gilbert's old house and a stack of straw and one of hay belonging to Houlden.'

Although the number of capital offences was now reduced, there was still an average of one hanging per week in England at this time. This case of arson was actually reported at some length in *The Times* because it represented the fears of landowners and farmers across the country. Richard Cooling and Thomas Motley set fire to a beast-shed and also a stack of straw. They were followed to Cooling's father's house where traces of their presence were found, and then to Stickney, where they were arrested.

The defence in court was that a beast-shed was not within the legal definition of an 'outhouse', and that the stack of straw was not by any means a 'stack', but this chop-logic desperation did not work. The judge also had details of earlier cases of arson committed by the men and they were sentenced to death. *The Times* reported that,

> The prisoners both acknowledged the justice of their punishment and by their demeanour showed that they had prepared their minds for the event. During the time of his confinement, Motley... acknowledged that it was their intention, before firing the stackyard... to have set fire to the premises of Mr Thimbleby of Kirby and Mr Kirkham of Hagnerby...

Even worse, when searched, Cooling was found to have a knife in the lining of his waistcoat.

The newspaper report then gave an account of their death:

> After the religious duties had been performed, both men shook hands with those around them, and ascended the scaffold without a murmur or any indication of fear. Whilst the executioner was drawing the cap over poor Motley's eyes and adjusting the rope, the brutally indifferent gaze of Cooling at the dreadful preparation was truly horrifying. He then underwent the same ordeal and about two minutes after twelve earthly justice was done and their souls were ushered into the presence of the Omniscience...

The judges' quarters, Lincoln. (Author's collection)

86

MURDER AT HECKINGTON

William Taylor, 18 March 1833

The ephemeral celebrity of hanged felons is well illustrated by this case. Around this time, Boston gaol was in neglect and ignored the reports of magistrates; a report noted that 'deterioration and corruption of the moral character must almost necessarily result from a confinement in a prison such as this.' In other words, criminality was hardly seen as remedied by rehabilitation, and the thought of that gaol was a deterrent, so there was violence and desperation in many attacks and thefts. The robbery committed by Taylor illustrates this desperation, but his trial and death were to become the subject of a broadside.

The printer in Silver Street, Lincoln, was out to exploit the hunger for crime stories amongst the general public, and William Taylor's imminent execution was a perfect example of the genre of the broadsheet murder story. The story, on one sheet, was adorned with a drawing of the 'new drop' at Cobb Hall and there was a ballad, stressing the horrible deed the villain had done on the Boston road:

> 'Several heavy blows he struck him, all on his head and side,
> Not time to make his peace with God before he groaned and died.'

The victim in question was William Burbank, who had been playing cards with the killer in a beer shop at Heckington on 9 March 1833. Burbank had a lot of cash on him on that occasion, and he went to the counter to buy beer with twenty or thirty shillings in his purse. Taylor was from Heckington, son of a carrier working between Sleaford and Boston. Although he was supposedly well respected, and father of three children, he had a wild younger brother. Something of that wildness was to emerge in William on this night. Burbank's friends knew about the purse and the money, and Burbank was heard to say that he was going home to clean up and have a shave. He left, and about half an hour later, Taylor left the beer house too.

A wine merchant named Nicholls found Burbank's body on the road the next morning at a quarter to six. A stake was lying near the body, but Nicholls was observant enough to see that it had not been taken from a fence nearby. He took the body to a surgeon at Heckington, and a constable went to the scene. Taylor had certainly been rash in his actions: two witnesses testified in court to meeting him that night. A rag-gatherer, Isaac Cooper, met him and asked where Taylor was going so late. He received no definite answer. A man named Hilton, who was a carpenter, was doing some shepherding work early in the day and he too saw Taylor. He also saw that there were several loose stakes in the place where Taylor was seen standing.

Poor Burbank had been attacked with real fury. The surgeon, Gibbs, reported that the skull was fractured, and that there was a hole in the forehead; his nose had been squashed flat and the bones totally crushed. His jaw had been broken and, overall, the large stake was the most likely weapon. When Taylor was arrested, there was no attempt to make up a story; he came clean and revealed that the purse, which had definitely been the reason for the attack, was lying at the spot where he killed Burbank. In Taylor's statement he

A Full, true and particular account of William Taylor, the unfortunate man who was Executed on the New Drop at Lincoln, on Monday the 18th March, 1833, for the wilful Murder of William Burbank, on the road from Sleaford to Boston, on Saturday the 9th March instant.

Give ear unto this horrid tale, good people far and near,
And of a barbarous murder, you presently shall hear,
Committed was on Sleaford road, the truth I will unfold;
A more cold blooded murder, scarce ever yet was told,

In Heckington one W. Taylor the murderer did dwell,
And likewise W. Burbanks, who by his hand has fell,
They had been drinking and gambling, its true what I impart,
And all that time this monster, had murder in his heart.

With cudgel in possession to Burbank then he came,
And stopped him on the road, his hands in blood to stain,
Several heavy blows he struck him, all on his head and side,
Not time to make his peace with God before he groaned & died.

To see the blood in streams to flow from Burbank's head,
You'd think it almost impossible so much for him to have bled,
But soon the villain was taken, and placed in a dreary cell,
For murdering poor Burbank as many a tongue can tell.

Now when his trial did come on, he at the bar did stand,
Like Moses he stood waiting, for the holy Lord's command,
The Judge when passing sentence made him this reply,
You're guilty of the murder, so prepare yourself to die.

You must prepare yourself to die, on Monday on the tree,
When hung the usual time thereon, buried you must be,
May these few lines a warning be, and prove to others good,
That they may ever shun the sin, of spilling precious blood.

William Taylor, aged 21, late of Heckington, laborer, charged by the Coroners inquest with the wilful murder of William Burbank, on the highway between Heckington and Sleaford, in the County of Lincoln.

William Brown keeps a beer shop at Heckington near Sleaford, the prisoner W. Taylor, W. Burbank, B. Medley, W. Nash and W. Cock, were at his house on Saturday the 9th day of March, W. Burbank came to witnesses house about half past two o'clock in the afternoon, he played two or three games at cards with the before mentioned W. Nash, W. Cook, and B. Medley, about 4 o'clock Burbank asked witness what time of day it was, witnesses wife told him it was somewhere about 4 o'clock, Burbank the deceased took out his purse to pay for two pints of ale, which he had lost, and said that he would go get shaved and then call that part of the town over as he went home, and immediately went out of the house; witness should know the purse again, it appeared to have about 20 or 30 shillings in it, the prisoner also saw the purse, prisoner remained about half an hour in the house after the deceased had left it, the rest of the party remained in the house until the prisoner returned about 7 o'clock in the evening. Prisoner said he would make one to play at cards for a quart, played 3 games, on the last game he said he would bet three pence on his game, he would have three pence for the ale, and said he would then go home. The prisoner remained until about nine o'clock, and was then taken into custody. Witness went on the following Monday morning, to a place called the scalp house in the church to see a dead body, it was the body of W. Burbank.

John Nichols is a Wine and Spirt Merchant, residing at Sleaford, he left Heckington on Saturday the 9th of March, to go to Sleaford at a quarter before six o'clock in the evening, about a mile and a quarter from Heckington he observed the body of a man laying on the road, he dismounted and went up to it, he lifted one hand up with his stick, the man appeared to be dead, but was quite warm, supposed it might have been an accident, but on turning round he observed a stake laying across the hedge, one end of which was very bloody, it was five or six yards from the body, it was day light, the stake could not have been taken from the adjoining hedge on which it was laying, witness has seen the stake since in possession of the constable of Heckington, witness immediately rode back to Heckington for Mr. Gibbs, a sugeon, they returned to the body together.

Isaac Cooper, is a rag gatherer, lives at Heckington, on Saturday the 9th inst. he went to Mr. Arnold's Mill near Heckington church, about half past five o'clock in the afternoon, met the prisoner W. Taylor, against the gate of the close in which the Mill stands, witness asked prisoner where he was going to at that time of night, prisoner said he did not know exactly just then, but afterwards said he was going a shepherding, prisoner was going Sleaford way, witness afterwards met W. Burbank about 40 yards after the prisoner, witness spoke to him, he appeared to be very little in liquor, was also going Sleaford way. Witness has since seen a dead body, it was the body of W. Burbank.

W. Hilton, is a carpenter at Heckington, left home on Saturday the 9th inst. about six o'clock to go a shepherding, to a close by the side of the turnpike road, leading from Heckington to Sleaford, he met the prisoner W. Taylor a little past six o'clock, a short distance from Heckington town end. Prisoner asked witness if he could tell him of a job. Witness knows Hilton's close, it is fenced with a quick hedge, it is three quarters of a mile from Heckington, part of the hedge is newly plashed, there are several loose stakes.

W. Gibbs, is a surgeon, residing at Heckington, Mr. Nichols came for witness shortly after six o'clock, on Saturday the 9th inst. to go with him to a place on the Sleaford road, where he found the body of a dead man, it was W. Burbank, examined the body, it was quite warm, and witness supposes it had not been dead more than quarter of an hour, the skull was fractured, a hole into which witness could get his finger, was perforated through the forehead into the brain, the lower part of the forehead was likewise destroyed, the nose was driven quite from its proper direction, the bones of which were literally crushed to atom, the lip was hanging down in a flap, the upper jaw was fractured, the back part of the head was cut, by blows from a round instrument, deceased died from the effects of those wounds, a large hedge stake is a likely instrument to cause such wounds. Witness was present when prisoner was apprehended, he denied his guilt. When the constable was going to lock prisoner up for the night, prisoner said he would tell all he knew about it, the prisoner said the purse was to be found near the spot where the body was found, on the other side of the road nearer to Heckington, the blood on the hedge stake was quite fresh, it was wet.

Charles Mastin is a Coroner for the County of Lincoln, and lives at Boston, he committed the prisoner, took the prisoner's examination, and cautioned him that any thing which prisoner might say would be brought as evidence against him. Mr. Mastin was here sworn to his signature, and the deposition of the prisoner was put in and read, it was to the following effect: that the prisoner and the deceased were walking on the road together, the deceased began to quarrel with prisoner about the cards and struck prisoner with his stick, prisoner returned the blow, deceased again struck the prisoner, prisoner then knocked deceased down and struck him two or three times, took from him his purse, emptied it of its contents, 2s. 7d. then threw the purse to the other side of the road, Burbank was not then dead, prisoner returned to Heckington, and on his way met W. Hilton, (as stated in Hilton's evidence above,) then went to the beer shop kept by W. Brown and played two or three games at cards, (as stated by that witness.)

J. Wilson is a Cooper, and lives at Heckington, went to the place where the murder was committed and a short distance from it and on the opposite side of the road he found a purse which he gave to John Robinson, chief constable of Sleaford.

Robert Squire is the constable of Heckington, and produced a bludgeon, which he had received from Mr. Gibbs a Surgeon. The bludgeon was a piece of white thorn about four feet long, and about the thickness of a man's wrist, the bark of one end was all bruised off and covered with blood, near the end a part of a branch remained, about three inches long, and as thick as a finger, which accounts for the hole through the forehead into the brain, as stated in the surgeon's evidence.

John Robinson, is a constable of Sleaford, and produced a purse, which he received from J. Wilson. W. Brown, the keeper of the beer shop, is then recalled, who swears that it is the identical purse, which he saw in the possession of W. Burbank, on the afternoon of Saturday, the 9th instant.

Mr. Gibbs, being recalled, stated that the wounds he had before described might be caused by the bludgeon now producing by the constable Squires, into whose possession witness gave it.—Mr. Squires, being asked whether the prisoner attempted to shake the crime off himself and place it on to others, he replied yes, the prisoner told him that he was innocent of the murder himself, but he could tell them who it was that had done it.

This was the case for the prosecution. The Learned Judge, then addressed the Jury at considerable length, recapitulated every minute circumstance that was given in evidence relative to this dreadful affair, making suitable comments as he proceeded in order to make every thing as plain and intelligible as possible, the gentlemen of the Jury appeared to pay every attention, and after recalling some of the witnesses to enquire into some trifling matters that did not appear exactly plain, and a few minutes consultation their Foreman with a down cast look, and a faltering tongue, pronounced a verdict of GUILTY; the Proclamation being delivered the Learned Judge proceeded to pass the awful sentence of Death on the prisoner, who maintained a sullen silence, his lordship addressed the prisoner at considerable length in an eloquent and solemn manner, commenting on the clearnes of the evidence, the magnitude of the crime being the greatest that one man can commit against his fellow man, and concluding by beseeching the prisoner to make the best use of the short time allowed him by law, to obtain pardon of his just and merciful God, through the merits of our Saviour Jesus Christ. He then sentenced him to be hanged, on Monday the 18th March instant, and his body to be buried within the precincts of the prison.

William Taylor was a native of Heckington near Sleaford, he has a father living, who has for many years followed the occupation of a carrier, between the Towns of Sleaford, Heckington, and Boston, he bears an unimpeachable character for honesty and sobriety, and is greatly respected by all who know him, we understand he has or rather had three sons, the elder of whom is we understand a very steady, excellent young man, in fact quite a religious character, the subject of this brief sketch, and his younger brother have for a considerable time led a life of dissipation, and have been almost a terror to the neighbourhood in which they lived.

EXECUTION.—The unfortunate man was conducted from his dreary cell and handed to the Executioner. Being pinioned he was conducted to the place of execution, where he suffered the awful penalty of the Law in the presence of a great number of Spectators, at the appointed time.

A broadside from 1833 detailing the hanging of William Taylor. (Lincolnshire Archives)

said that the two of them had walked together and fallen out; they had argued about the earlier gambling at the beer house. Taylor said that Burbank had provoked him, hitting him with his stick, and that in retaliation he had knocked the man to the ground. The surgeon's evidence and the examination of the stake (the 'bludgeon' as it was called) led to one conclusion. The judge apparently spent some time in sermonising in a solemn tone on what had happened, and then everyone present waited for the foreman of the jury to speak.

The broadsheet writer noted that the foreman had a downcast look and spoke falteringly as he uttered the word, 'Guilty'. The judge sentenced the prisoner to be hanged on Monday 18 March, 'and his body to be buried within the precincts of the prison.' His last moments of life as he walked from his miserable cell were spent being stared at by a massive crowd, as he was the centre of attraction for that day. It seems that the expected speech and repentance were not forthcoming.

87

HANGED FOR TWO SHILLINGS

William Stephenson, 22 March 1833

The calendar of prisoners for the 1833 Lent assizes records the bare facts: 'William Stephenson, alias Beckett, aged 21 ... charged with stealing a black cart mare, the property of E. Buck.' He had also attacked a man named John Shepherd as he rode home late at night after drinking at a public house in Burgh-le-Marsh in 1833. Stephenson set about him with a club and was too powerful for his victim.

The attacker severely wounded Shepherd and then robbed him of a watch and some cash – just two shillings to be precise. But this was a desperate and clumsy attack because the victim came round and raised the alarm, and boot prints led directly to the attacker's lodgings: police work was never easier! Stephenson and a colleague, Pearson, were involved and of the two it was Stephenson who had committed the violence so he was to die, whereas his accomplice was transported for life.

88

RAPIST FOUND WITH
A BLOODY FACE

Thomas Knapton, 26 July 1833

Frances Elston ran home in a distressed state on 30 June 1833, shouting for help. She had been raped by a young man on the road to Gainsborough; but the rapist had talked about himself, and Frances had information to pass on. He was found in Gainsborough that same night in an attic, with blood on his face.

Mr Justice Taunton presided at the Summer assizes. The man's youth was of no consideration, and Knapton, just seventeen, was sentenced to death. His parents came to see him, and several statements about how he had been corrupted by drink and bad company followed. There was earnest prayer and remorse. But naturally, despite the crime, such a young felon aroused a certain degree of feeling and there was a very large attendance at his hanging. The young man obliged them by praying long and hard before the noose was placed around his neck.

The body was taken by the family for burial. It was to be the last hanging in the city for a crime other than murder. Attitudes to the death penalty were slowly changing.

89

ROBBERY WITH VIOLENCE

Thomas Johnson, 17 March 1843

Thomas Johnson, who went by various other names, came from Burton-upon-Trent and was a reckless character. He broke into Elizabeth Evinson's home in February 1843 and tied up both Elizabeth and her sister; both were old ladies, Elizabeth being seventy years old. He wanted to steal whatever he could and decided to keep the two women still and out of his way, so he chose the method of tying them to their bed and covering them over with the bedclothes. After that he stole silver and cash.

Whatever his intention was, Johnson brought about their deaths, because they suffocated. He admitted that his death sentence for murder was just, but denied any desire to take the victims' lives. That seems to be a contradiction, but it is in keeping with the perverse and meaningless actions he committed in the course of his crimes, and this time he took a step too far; if nothing else, a sheer lack of common sense is at the heart of the case, as he must have realised that doing such a thing to these frail and elderly women was likely to endanger their lives.

90

A BOSTON POISONING

Eliza Joyce, 2 August 1844

The *Lincolnshire Chronicle* for 2 August 1844 relates the sad tale of a thirty-one-year-old woman who walked to the scaffold, pausing as she did so to 'bid a lingering farewell to the bright world which she had sacrificed.' Eliza Joyce wore a black dress and carried a prayer book; some said that her features had an expression of ghastly agony. The massive crowd gathered as usual, trying to push their way to find a good spot for watching the high drama of the hanging. They would have seen the all-too familiar procession of prisoner, chaplain, bailiffs and hangman. The man with the task of seeing that Eliza was hanged as quickly as possible was William Calcraft, the national executioner. One reporter said that, 'The effect of her appearance on the immense crowd was awfully striking – a profound stillness reigned through the living mass.'

What had she done to deserve this? Eliza had poisoned her son, William, her daughter, Ann, and also her stepdaughter, Emma. She confessed to these crimes in Boston workhouse, telling the master about it after she and her husband had separated.

A print showing the easy availability of poisons. (Punch)

William Calcraft.
(Author's collection)

She had married William Joyce, being his second wife, in Boston in 1840, and they had lived an ordinary life. But after giving birth to William and finding that he was weak and sickly; she had become immersed in what today we would call a puerperal depression. This is evident from her later explanations about what she had done. She bought some arsenic, but her husband had not wanted her to: the implication being that the man had some sort of notion that she was dangerous to herself or her own kin in her current mood. He found out that she had been given arsenic instead of nux vomica, and then he realised that half of the packet she bought was missing. Their son, William, then became seriously sick with all the signs of arsenic poisoning.

William made a statement about the poison and the illness, and Eliza was arrested. Her son, William, died that Christmas, 1842. At the Summer Assizes she was acquitted, as there was doubt about whether or not the whole business had been accidental. In her confession in the workhouse, the first killing, of her baby girl, was weighing heavily on her conscience and she told how she had bought three pennyworth of laudanum and given it to little Emma, who had died quickly after that. She said, plaintively, in explanation of this when the workhouse master asked her why she had done these awful things, 'I don't know, except I thought it was such a troublesome thing to bring a family of children into this troublesome world.' Her emotional state, and her husbands' fears about the arsenic, become understandable when he noted that she said that she was 'so burdened that she could not live, and hoped that, as she had confessed, she should be better.'

In her third trial in Lincoln in 1844, she was charged with two murders. She had basically been afraid of having a large family and the responsibility that went with it.

That was the route to the gallows. Calcraft adjusted the rope and as Old Tom chimed midday, she fell into eternity; she died, the press reported, without a struggle. Eliza Joyce was the last woman in England to be hanged for a murder to which she had confessed and pleaded guilty.

Old Tom, whose bell chimed on execution day. (Author's collection)

91

A WAINFLEET MURDER

John Ward, 27 July 1849

John Ward was living with his mother at Thorpe when he started to become overly familiar with a servant girl, Susan Bogg. His mother gave him an ultimatum for good behaviour, but that was not the end of the matter. Ward was simmering with discontent. On the afternoon of 9 April, as the family sat down, John went for his gun and then threatened to take his own life or that of another. He went out, but on his return his mother commanded him to get to work, but he refused.

Later, he came in again, as both women were still in the sitting room, and he shot his mother. He had experienced a breakdown of some kind, and tried to persuade Susan to run away with him. He then tried to take his own life. The alarm was raised and he was apprehended and brought to justice; he had a date with the judge and jury at Lincoln. There was a desperate attempt to state that the shooting was accidental but that failed, and Ward was sentenced to hang.

There was a massive crowd out in the streets for this hanging. The local newspaper reported:

> On Tuesday morning the chaplain was early with the unfortunate man, and preached to him and the other prisoners an affecting sermon. The crowds of people rushing into Lincoln were immense; steamboats, railway carriages, wagons, carts, gigs etc. were all wedged full and before the hour of execution [12 o'clock] every point commanding a view of the gallows was occupied by a large mob.

In fact, so crazed was this mass of people that an overloaded vessel coming into Lincoln from Boston had nearly stuck fast in the river and the people had to get out and walk the rest of the way.

Readers were told that the hangman at Lincoln then earned '£5 for executing a male and for executing a female, £6; and is entitled to the clothes of the parties if he thinks fit to have them.'

92

THE OLD MAN PUT UP
A FIGHT

Henry Carey & William Picket, 5 August 1859

At its simplest level, this is a story about two young men with plenty of drink in them, desperate for money, who set out to rob and kill a man. But they were to go down in criminal history as the last people to be hanged in public in the county.

By the 1850s, there was an increasing unease among many in Victorian society about the nature of hanging and its processes and traditions. In 1833, an anonymous author, simply described as a schoolmaster who had worked in Newgate, wrote a book with a long discourse on hangings; he had seen many, and on the subject of its being public, he wrote:

> It is then asked may not some tendency for cruel laws originate in a love of excitement, and particularly of that excitement which shares the distress of others... I am quite at a loss to account for the number of respectable persons who consent to be brought to witness the horrible scenes... Sometimes the affair takes on quite another turn, and the malefactor is seized with a frenzy for death, as being the only road to happiness. This effect is brought on by the operation of great excitement on weak minds...

There was certainly 'great excitement... on weak minds' on 5 August 1859 in Lincoln, when Henry Carey and William Picket were hanged. But the murderous tale begins one night in March 1859 at the Ship Inn in Sibsey. Sixty-four year old William Stevenson had been in Boston that day and was enjoying a drink. In the pub at the same time were Carey and Picket, two young men in need of cash. They were talking about their miserable condition, the fact that the world seemed to be unfair to them, and the more they drank, the more the possibility of remedying the situation seemed to be possible if they were rash enough. The next stage was to choose a victim, and there in the bar was William, a man who had made some money selling pigs. The idea was first expressed by Carey, who said, 'Let's kill the old bastard, I think he's got some money.' They left the Ship Inn before Stevenson, with a plan to ambush him.

A woman near the river the next morning saw what she first thought was a shirt floating in the ditch of a sewer, only a short distance from the old man's cottage. As she approached, however, she saw that it was the bloody body of William. He had terrible injuries to his head.

The narrative of the attack had clear traces: the police found a trail of blood where the victim had either been dragged or had been walking as blood dripped from him. There were even some blood-marked fence stakes and footprints nearby. There was going to be no problem making an arrest, as people had seen the two men – they had a local reputation as rough characters – the night before. When the police found them, there was blood on one man's boot, and a direct match of their boots with the prints in the mud. Carey even had Stevenson's knife in his pocket. They had beaten the man viciously with the stakes and then thrown him into a ditch. But he was not so easy to kill; Stevenson climbed out of the ditch and horrified them. They had to finish the job, and that was exceptionally brutal; after all, they knew him and he knew them; his last words to them were, 'Oh Picket, what are you doing?'.

All this had been done on the expectation of stealing a large amount of money, but the man only had a sovereign on him. Picket, in court, said that had he known that, he would have let him pass. But the attack had been planned while the two men were full of beer, and were game to drink even more, with three pints being put into a jug for them by the landlord before they left. Carey had been the one to conceive of the attack, and he had talked Picket into doing it. That was the beginning of the design on the old man's life: the belief that he had a few pounds on him; that it would be an easy thing to accomplish, and the drink had filled them with reckless bravado.

Carey and Picket were drifters, men with a reliance on either short-lived casual labour or petty crime; their bed for the night on this occasion was an old boat, and no doubt they were taking some more beer out with them to make sure they had a night's sleep through such discomfort. In court, as questions were asked to obtain more detail about the events of that night, it emerged that Carey had put a lot of thought into the crime. He had said, 'Threepence is all I've got. I must have some money from somewhere.' The two had started quarrelling as they became more drunk, and eventually the landlord told them that they had drunk enough and should be going home. Then, when Picket had said that the old man knew him, Carey was ready with something he had prepared earlier: two handkerchiefs, one with two holes in for Picket to see through. He was not known to Stevenson, so he was not concerned. If there was any doubt about whether or not Carey had indulged in premeditation, it was clarified when these words were spoken at the trial: 'Let's go round by the bridge over the dyke...'. He knew exactly where the best place would be to wait for the victim. He went on to size up the situation and the likely defence: 'He keeps a good big walking stick; you'll have to hold him while I do the rest.' When Picket said he would not hold the old man, it became obvious that Carey was ready for a fight and knew that he could not lose.

Stevenson was a strong self-reliant man, well respected in the area. He was at that time living with his son at Sibsey Northlands. This isolated place was described by one reporter at the time as 'so called because the lands are intersected by drains, some large and some small, running in various directions.' It was a long, bare stretch of land and water back then. One story told in the 1930s about Sibsey was that the road was so monotonous and uninteresting that a man driving a coach in the 1860s when the roads were deep and watery, asked a local what place was this? He was sold Stickney and said, 'we shall all come to Stick neck next!' He lived at a house just 500yds from the bridge that the two villains had crossed that night. There was no fence between the road and the sewer on the path to Stevenson's home.

Stevenson was certainly not drunk; he was walking homewards when he saw the two figures by the side of the path. This was the point at which they made their first attack, with the stakes. One stake shattered into pieces, such was the fury of the killers. Then they threw him into the ditch, and when he came out, coughing and groaning, they must have had a fright, thinking they have battered him to death. But he had been temporarily revived by the cold water; it is not clear whether he realised who they were and what exactly had happened to him. But it was Picket who ran to him and gave the *coup de grace*. He was searched and robbed; they found that he had just a sovereign on him and some more change; Picket took that, along with the knife and Carey had the sovereign. They then hid the booty in a hole back nearby the Sun Inn. Close by, the drunkards then slept. They did not even stagger towards the boat they had in mind.

Stevenson had been very severely battered; when Mary Semper found the body and called in her husband and then the forces of law, it was a shocking sight before them in the sewer ditch. Mr Semper and a man named Coates dragged the body out of the water for closer inspection. The scene of crime was described in this way by a reporter from the area:

> At about 80 yard's distance from the place where the body was found, but on the opposite side of the road, were seen indications of a struggle, trodden grass with blood upon it, and footmarks were observed, apparently made by persons crossing the road, and at the same time dragging with them something heavy in the ditch that skirted the road were found three broken fragments of a hedge stake marked with drops of blood and in the low hedge that bounded the sewer mud was noticed, which seemed to have been made by someone getting over it. The hedge was broken down and wet and in one part bloody about a foot's breadth.

Other fragments of a stake in the water were put together and made a stake over 4ft long. There were blood and hair on the grass by the side of the sewer. It was the old man's son who had the misfortune to come across a pool of blood, about 12yds from the hedge, in towards the field. A Sergeant James took control of things and soon found that the two men sleeping by George Sands's place were the suspects. It looked as though they had attacked and robbed the old man, attempted to drown him in the sewer ditch to be sure that he was dead; then, as the marks of the struggle clearly conveyed the sequence of events, there had been increasing desperation as the man proved to be an indomitable opponent.

Carey had said to Picket, when he planned the walk across the bridge to the place of ambush, 'That's what I wanted you for.' In other words, the 'malice aforethought' was meticulous, and even in drink the idea was expressed clearly. But at the Crown Court of the Midland Circuit, Fitzjames Stephen for the prosecution made it explicit from the start that both were equally to blame: *The Times* reported that:

> After a few introductory remarks, he stated to the jury the facts by which the case on the part of the Crown would be conducted... commented with great minuteness upon a statement made by the prisoner Picket... tended to show that Picket himself was present upon the spot when the deceased, Stevenson, was by some persons attacked and killed.

It soon became apparent that this prelude to the case was because Picket had been advised by his defence counsel, Mr Macaulay and Mr Flowers, to push blame towards Carey, who was in fact undefended. Picket's long statement in the dock was biased towards showing Carey as the originator of the murderous plan, and made Picket himself seem like a weak, docile figure who was more susceptible than ever when he had taken a few pints of ale.

Carey was silent throughout the trial and never asked a single question of anyone. His account of the day reinforces the view of the two men as being rootless and subject to the whims of the employers around them: Picket had told how he worked for Mr Sands for a few days, staying with him, and that he would be locked out if he did not leave the Sun by a certain time. It had been market day and plenty of people were drinking after a long day's work. Was Picket an accomplice, or an accessory after the fact? For a long time on 27 July he spoke at length about how he was advised at Stickney, when first arrested, to say nothing; that he was a passive individual who had been easily led by a more aggressive and wayward character. If Carey was angry, and had to stand in court and hear all this from a 'grass', then he was impressively self-controlled.

The defence lawyers were amazingly active in their efforts to ease their client's condition and how he was portrayed in the court. They even said that if common justice regarding the circumstantial evidence incriminated him, then 'they should also give consideration to other things that tended to limit the degree of his criminality.' By this they meant that there were suggestions that Stevenson had used Picket harshly in the past, and that Stevenson's nature had perhaps been made more unpleasant that some might think, as he had been given notice to quit from his previous property. All this was very complicated and smacks of being a desperate last-ditch attempt to find any vestige of sympathy for

Picket that might just have been possible. If there was doubt about Picket, then there was none about Carey, at least in the mind of the *Lincolnshire Chronicle* reporter, who wrote that Carey had 'a low forehead, thought to distinguish murderers.'

Another factor was the atmosphere in the court at Lincoln. It was a particularly hot and humid day on the first day of the trial; the jury, having to listen to all this detail and speculation in order that they might compare the two men and begin to see some differences, was under stress. The judge, Mr Justice Williams, adjourned the trial until the next day and the jurors were escorted around the corner to the White Hart Hotel for the night.

The next day, matters were soon brought to a close. It took the jury just twenty-five minutes to make a decision. Both men were found guilty. When sentenced, Picket said, 'My father has often told me that if I kept company with Carey I should be transported or hanged.' It is particularly ironic that he also made a point of saying how much he had liked the victim: 'It is all drink... Mr Stevenson was always a friend to me. He took me in when I was turned out of my own house.' Carey then confessed that he was really responsible for urging Picket to be involved. But none of this mattered; they were to be hanged by Calcraft.

On the day of execution it was noted that they fully confessed their guilt and 'manifested the greatest repentance.' This last public execution in the county was perhaps the worst example of the public hysteria and gruesome fascination with the drama of the scaffold. There were disgraceful scenes at the event, on 5 August 1859. One of the most irritating developments in the minds of the local reformists was that the landlords of two public houses nearby in Bailgate, the Plough Inn and the Yarborough Arms, made their front yards into viewing areas, with an admission charge of threepence for those citizens who wanted a good view of the Cobb Hall tower, from where the two men would be suspended. The writer for the *Lincolnshire Chronicle* expressed his disgust:

> It is almost impossible to believe that men following a respectable position in society would be guilty of so discreditable an act and that men could be found to patronise them. But so it was, and judging from the numerous persons who paid their three pence, we have no doubt the landlords made a considerable sum of money. Before twelve o'clock every spot where a sight of the gallows could be obtained was filled with a crowd so dense that it was almost impossible to penetrate through it.

Today it is hard to imagine, as a building development of shops and restaurants by the castle car park now obscures the view, but as the visitor walks from the car park through to Bailgate, he walks beneath Cobb Hall, and the projecting spar of stone may still be seen from the centre of the tower. In 1859 there would have been a flat stretch of land between what is now a preserved Roman pavement in the Bail all the way to the corner of Cobb Hall by the castle fortifications. It would have been a very large open area, enough to hold thousands of spectators. Around that area in 1859 the crowd packed in, to gaze upwards, listen to any dying speeches, and take a voyeuristic pleasure in seeing the two murderers hang.

This event was the end of a very long tradition in English society. We now have, with hindsight, a clear documentation of the varieties of execution ritual. Some commentators saw these affairs as an opportunity for repentance and an assertion of faith. When there was no religious content, men of the cloth were not happy, as in Lincoln on this occasion when a local clergyman tried to exhort the noisy crowd to a more sober and appropriate behaviour. He went on record in the newspaper as saying, 'There is generally much drinking, bad language and thoughtlessness, and cruel laughter when the unhappy criminals are punished.' He had an explanation: that sinful men 'cannot bear to look calmly at so awful a sight as the death of a fellow creature so they excite themselves as if they were at a place of amusement.'

The other aspect of the scaffold tradition was the rebellion. In street literature and song, the notion of the unrepentant criminal, the man who puts two fingers up to the law, always had a place. Robert Burns' song, 'Macpherson's Farewell', expresses this in the lines:

> There's some have come to see me die,
> some to hear me play.
> But Macpherson's time will ne'er be lang
> On yonder gallows tree.
> So rantingly, so dauntingly played he...

This is the paradox in mid-Victorian Britain, and it could be seen that day in Lincoln: the old public spectacle as in the days of Jack Sheppard and the parade to Tyburn, in which defiance, not repentance, was the order of the day, was still persistent, and it clashed with the aspirations and radical ideas of Victorian religion and philanthropy. Though it is interesting to point out here that even Thomas Hardy, when he was sixteen (in 1856) watched the public execution of Martha Brown, and as Robert Gittings relates: 'In 1919, with Lady Ilchester and daughter, he recounted the terrible details, told him by an ancestor, of the burning of Mary Channing, the murderess...'.

But as for Carey and Picket, their deaths were unremarkable. There were no scenes of high drama, no defiance. It was something of a paradox, with the shameful scenes at this event, to recall that the executioner, William Calcraft, had also profited from the business and violence of public hangings by selling pies at these events to make money. But he made a success of his career, being paid £1 a week retaining fee by the City of London and over £5 retaining fee from Surrey. He was to retire in 1874. Oliver Cyriac explains the contribution made by this man to the rituals of the trade: 'Calcraft hanged people off a three-foot drop, and indulged in one of the more peculiar ruses to segregate his personal life from his professional life. On arrival at a prison for a hanging garbed in a black suit, he would change his clothes, donning another black suit of identical design...'.

Only three years before this last execution in Lincoln, a Royal Commission recommended the ending of this degrading spectacle; that panel of professionals saw that any deterrent effect such punishment might have was far outweighed by the dangers and social problems generated by the attendance of large crowds. The last public execution in England took place in Newgate on 26 May 1868. Another factor which helps to explain the many expressions of the barbarity of the deaths of Picket and Carey is the radical change in the law which was to take place just two years after their deaths. This was the Offences Against the Person Act of 1861. This legislation meant that the death penalty was abolished for all crimes except murder and High Treason.

93

A CONTROVERSIAL HANGING

Priscilla Biggadike, 28 December 1868

In 1868 the village of Mareham-le-Fen, around six miles south of Horncastle, was a small parish close to Wildmore fen; the population at that time was about 480, and listed as notable residents in the 1850s were fifteen general retailers and seventeen butchers.

In other words, it was a place where people scraped together whatever living they could, many existing close to the level of what was then called the 'underclass' – a term embracing many categories of person from poacher to general casual labourer.

Such a family group was that of Richard and Priscilla Biggadike. Priscilla was born in Gedney and married Richard in 1855. In 1868 they were existing in a ramshackle hut at Stickney; she was twenty-nine and her husband a year older. They had three children, but also two lodgers: George Ironmonger and Thomas Proctor. The latter was a rat-catcher (they were often employed by the corporation at a set fee per tail). All lived under the same small roof, using two beds just eighteen inches apart. Ironmonger was in the habit of taking Mr Biggadike's place in the marital bed when he went out to work. Naturally, problems arose from this. There were domestic arguments and altercations as time went on and there was a suspicion that the last child born to them, in 1868, was Proctor's.

Imagining the people involved here, and the way they lived, evokes a picture of hardship and strife; village people speaking about them later said that they often quarrelled. Richard Biggadike was usually out at work all day, and his wife left with the chores and her isolation.

This element of the narrative is important: a moment's reflection on Priscilla's life arguably plays a part in assessing her situation and how she must have had to behave in such circumstances. What never really emerged from the investigations was the nature of this liaison with the lodger. His sexual attentions were more than likely forced upon her. The whole social context suggests a whole range of stresses and strains on the woman at the centre of this *ménage a trios*, and how she would have had to work every waking minute to feed, clothe and support these men. After all, they were all living at the basest level, hand-to-mouth and in a condition of extreme deprivation.

On 30 September 1868, Biggadike ate a meal of hot cakes and mutton, made by Priscilla. He took to his bed mortally ill, and died after eleven hours of agonising pain and retching. There was no doubt in the doctor's mind at the inquest that this was a case of arsenic poisoning. Obviously, Priscilla switched the focus to Proctor, saying that she had seen him put a powder into the food. Mr Biggadike was taking a medicine already, and the powder was also added to this, she claimed. Her story became more convoluted and when Proctor was shown to have no motive for doing such a thing, a Grand Jury found him innocent and there were only Priscilla's allegations to put against him.

The situation was compounded by her account of Richard having stated that he wanted to end his own life; he had large debts, and she said that she had found a suicide note written by him. But here was a slip: her husband could not read or write. A reported statement by Priscilla, 'I cannot abide him. I should like to see him brought home dead', was the most conclusive point made by the prosecution. There had been violent and frequent quarrels between the married pair, and that was part of the case as well.

The inquest, held on 3 October, heard a statement from Dr Maxwell, saying that he was called to the home at seven in the evening on the 30 September, and that he 'found him [Richard] in great pain in bed, sick and violently purged. He had all the symptoms of poisoning by some irritant.' At a post-mortem examination conducted by the same doctor the next morning, he confirmed death by poison and was convinced that arsenic had been used, and in a very large dose. 'There was enough left in the body,' he commented, 'to destroy the life of another person. I never saw a clearer case of death by poison.'

Priscilla had been placed in the House of Correction, where she had a miserable time: the place was reported as having 'offensively unhealthy cells ten feet by eight… the only admittance of light is through a tiny niche in the wall.' She went to talk to the Governor, John Farr Phillips, and there she implicated Proctor. Her words seem precise and detailed, at least on the surface:

> On the last day of September I was standing against the tea table, and saw Thomas Proctor put a white powder of some sort into a teacup, and then he poured some milk, which stood upon the table, into it. My husband came into the room directly after and, and I poured his tea out, and he drank it, and more besides…

Folkingham House of Correction, the first holding cell for many under arrest. (Author's collection)

She then gave more information about Proctor putting something else into Richard's medicine bottle. She then tested it: 'As soon as he left the room I poured some medicine into the cup and gave it to my husband, and tasted it myself. In an hour afterwards I was sick, and I was sick for two days after…'.

All this is peculiarly confusing, as her actions do not seem entirely logical. She went on to say more about Proctor, to such an extent that Superintendent Wright of Spilsby charged Proctor with the murder, who in turn stated his innocence. Priscilla added the information about the suicide note, saying that she had burned it. When Wright insisted that Richard was illiterate, she said, 'No, someone must have done it for him.' Most of her statements are very difficult to uphold, and the general manner of her delivery of this material only built the case against her more strongly. This tiny detail is the one note about Priscilla that has persisted to this day. Tours in Lincoln Castle now have a script for the guide to say in which the public are informed that Priscilla made this 'fatal mistake' about the illiteracy of her husband. But someone may well have 'written it for him.' In the circumstances, if this was a suicide, a man would genuinely want the people left behind to understand, and even suffer some guilt and remorse.

But all this contemporary thinking had no bearing on the case. Things were seen as much more straightforward. The jury did not take long to return a guilty verdict of wilful murder against both defendants. They were both committed to attend Lincoln Assizes, and were taken to the House of Correction in the meantime. Priscilla was refused any bail.

At the assize trial, Mr Justice Byles presided and although he noted the circumstantial evidence, he expressed his certainty of the simplicity of the case and the obvious guilt of the prisoner. He asked the jury why they recommended mercy and they simply said that it was that there were 'circumstantial grounds.' Clearly, he took no notice of this opinion. Proctor was acquitted and the case went on relentlessly against Priscilla. All Proctor had really said was that he was a rat-catcher and that he kept ferrets: a one-dimensional man whose nature was never really examined. All the focus was on Priscilla. The *Lincolnshire Chronicle* reported that, 'She showed not the slightest emotion throughout the hearing of the trial, and she only made a small show of grief when the sentence was passed on her.'

George Ironmonger had tried to visit her but was refused; some of her own family did see her but could not talk her into admitting guilt. We have a great deal of information about her time in gaol and of her execution. She was attended by a chaplain, Revd W.H. Richter, and he was with her most of the time until the hour appointed for the execution: 9 a.m. on the morning of 28 December 1868.

Walking out, she wore a white cap and black gown, stockings and boots. She made a moaning noise all the time she walked. The hanging was to be out of the public eye, on a scaffold by the County Hall, where the chaplain asked her, 'Do you still persist in your declaration of innocence and have you anything to do with the crime in thought, word or deed?'

Priscilla simply replied, 'No, I have not Sir.'

She was, in the words of Richter, 'left to God' without repentance. *The Times* (on 29 December) gave a rather different report to that of the local press:

> On finally parting with the Governor and chaplain she shook hands with them. The governor asked her whether she admitted the justice of her sentence. She murmured something – one of the warders thought it was an affirmative reply – but the precise words could not be heard. A few seconds before she had exclaimed, 'Oh! You won't hang me!' Everything being in readiness the executioner proceeded to complete his task.

When the Minster clock, Big Tom, struck the hour, the bolt was slid out and the trap lowered. Thomas Askern, the hangman from York, had been inefficient. He was in the habit of tying the knot under the chin, not at the side under the ear. Askern was to hang the infamous Mary Ann Cotton in Durham four years after this visit to Lincoln, and just a few months before this Lincoln job, he had hanged a teenager in Dumfries. Priscilla Biggadike took three minutes to die. Her last words were reputedly, 'Surely all my troubles are over!'.

There had been a Capital Punishment Amendment Act in 1868, and this case followed hard on that, and so some of the new rules about execution procedure were meticulously followed, the most dramatic being the ritualistic nature of some of the guidelines: 'The bell of the prison or the bell of the parish church... to be tolled for fifteen minutes before and fifteen minutes after the execution' and 'A black flag to be hoisted at the moment of execution.' Lincoln was provided with all these trappings of a formal state execution.

The epilogue to this case was what everyone concerned must have feared: the hanged woman was innocent. In 1882, on his deathbed, Thomas Proctor confessed to the murder. Unfortunately, this fact has not permeated popular history. In the 1970s, three accounts of the story were in print, and these give great emphasis to the simplicity of the poisoning element and motives for the wife to kill the husband. These accounts focus on the common use of poisons at the time and Priscilla's use of them:

> another woman who had been offered arsenic – which she called white mercury – to kill mice by Priscilla four months before Biggadike's death. Proctor... had visited this woman after the death and warned her, 'Mind what you say.' To which she had replied, 'Do you think I'm a fool that knows naught?'

Clearly, this kind of writing, making it seem as though Priscilla was some kind of local expert on killing vermin, can make her seem exceptional. In fact, she was no different to any other country wife. Using poison would have been common practice, and local druggists would no doubt bend the law with regard to retailing arsenic when they were selling regularly to familiar faces.

But all this has no bearing on the execution. The event is told briefly in this paragraph from Ward's *Historical Guide to Lincoln* (1880):

> 1868 Dec. 28th
> Priscilla Biggadike, for the murder of her husband by poisoning on the 1st October. This wretched murderess was the first that was hung under the Private Executions Act, which was strictly adhered to, the officials of the prison and four reporters being the only persons present, beside the chaplain, sheriff and Askern the executioner. She protested her innocence to the last.

The grave of Priscilla Biggadike.
(Author's collection)

From the tower of the castle the black flag was raised. One coda to the story is that a warder, Mary Fox, had given Priscilla a handkerchief as the sentence was passed on her. Long after the case, when Fox was visiting Madame Tussaud's, Priscilla Biggadike's effigy was there with a handkerchief in the hand: it was the one Fox had given her prisoner.

94

THE MURDEROUS BREWER

William Horry, 1 April 1872

William Horry's family came from Boston, but he was something of a wanderer, leaving for Staffordshire with his new wife in 1866. But he left his family and took to the road, eventually returning to Boston, and then living in Nottingham. His wife then came to live in Boston and one day Horry's jealousy about his wife led to him coming to Boston, gun in hand, to kill her, and indeed he did.

In January 1872, at his father's house, he shot dead his wife, Jane. There was no doubt that the act had been premeditated, and at the trial it was clear that this was a murder case. He was sentenced to hang. In fact, this hanging was the very first job carried out by the famous Horncastle hangman, William Marwood. He was now in a position to actually use the 'long drop' – a more humane method of hanging which he conceived and practised by using the weighing and dropping of sacks.

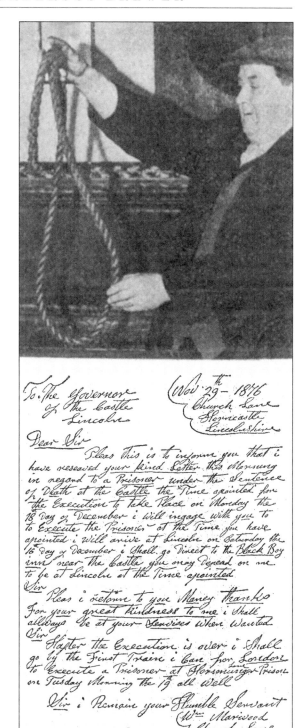

Marwood's ropes. A letter from
Marwood to the governor of Lincoln
Castle accepting a commission.
(Author's collection)

95

HE KILLED HIS SWEETHEART

Peter Blanchard, 9 August 1875

Peter Blanchard was a Louth tanner, and the love of his life was twenty-two-year-old Louise Hodgson. They had been courting for some years and were engaged in 1875, but jealousy was to come between them. A friend of his family, a man named Campion, was becoming a rival for the affections of the young lady, and one day, when Louise and Campion were on their way to a service at the Methodist chapel, Blanchard confronted his rival and threatened him; he walked with them for a while but then went home to fetch a knife.

At the home of the Hodgson family, Louise and Campion were sitting down when Blanchard came in with his knife. Thinking they should sort it out between them, Blanchard was left alone with Louise. A row escalated and a scream was heard; when relatives rushed to the scene Jane told them, 'I've been stabbed!' She died of her wounds and Blanchard said he was glad of that, and that, in his own words, he would 'Die like a man for her.' He did just that, being sentenced to hang at the Lent assizes, in spite of the defence's attempt to show that Blanchard was insane. He died to the accompaniment of a thunderstorm.

96

CAUGHT IN LOWESTOFT

William Clarke, 26 March 1877

William Clarke and three friends were poaching pheasants at Eagle wood in the January of this year. The four men split into two pairs, Clarke going with a man named Garner to Norton Disney.

Henry Walker and his assistants were looking for poachers when they saw Clarke and Garner pass by. After being told to stop, Clarke decided to challenge the keepers and showed his gun, but they were pursued when they ran, and Clarke turned to shoot the pursuers. He shot Walker dead. Of course, the poachers were known; they had been seen. They were rounded up, except for Clarke, who had left the area. This then became a work for the detectives and Superintendent Brown, of Kesteven, doggedly followed his man until he finally cornered him in Lowestoft. With the help of backup, the killer was arrested – just a short period before he was to sail for the continent.

All the poachers were on trial in Lincoln on 7 March, and there, Garner identified Clarke as the killer. Marwood had another job; Clarke was hanged and the others acquitted.

Owston Ferry.
(Author's collection)

97

FIRST HANGING IN THE
NEW PRISON

James Anderson, 19 February 1883

James Anderson was a man with a violent temper and a rabid hatred of his wife. His brutal slaying of her at their home in East Ferry led him to the gallows. The story begins with James as pub landlord in Owston Ferry, and life with his wife, Mary, seems to have been difficult to say the least. It is clear that he was always nasty to her, and that he was a short-tempered, testy man. He was physically aggressive, and at a time when wives were particularly vulnerable. In late-Victorian England no one knew too much about 'stress' or even the psychology behind acts of physical brutality.

On 6 December came the fatal day for Mary. Their nephew, John Wood, had moved over the water to live with the son, and when he came over to pick up some clothes, he found that there was a major row in progress. Mary was shouting accusations of infidelity and James was obviously being inflamed into a rage. He grabbed a knife and set on her, with Mary running out into the kitchen shouting, 'Murder!'.

John found them grappling on the kitchen floor. Then he saw his aunt staggering out, bleeding at the neck. She fell down, leaving a trail of blood behind her. James then turned the blade on himself, dragged the blade across his throat. He was ranting that all this hell was down to Mary for provoking him. But he was destined not to die on that bloody floor. James recovered, was arrested and shut up in gaol. When his brother went to visit him, he simply said, 'If the judge was to ask for a reprieve for me, I would ask him not to, for I want to die for it.' Anderson was the first man to die at the new prison on Greetwell Road. Marwood, the hangman, had by this time become notorious for the execution of the murderers linked to the infamous Phoenix Park assassinations of 1882, and now he put an end to the miserable life of Anderson.

98

IRISH JOE HANGS

Thomas Garry, 7 May 1883

Thomas Garry was known as Irish Joe, and he lodged with John Newton at Sleaford. In February 1882 they fell out. Garry went to stay at a local pub (the Wheel), but he had murderous thoughts in his head. A neighbour named Farmer went to feed his animals one morning and called in to see Newton. He found the man on the floor with his throat cut and a gunshot wound.

Garry had been out of the pub for a while and he knew that the forces of law would soon be looking for him, so he tried to sort out some alibis, but it was no use. He was arrested at the pub and could only say that he had been in the pub at the time of the killing. But the details of the crime scene made it a simple matter to link Irish Joe to the murder. Money had been stolen, and it was known that Garry was very hard up; there was blood and brick dust on Garry's boots that matched the scene traces, and it was found that the witnesses Garry had at the pub were committing perjury. He was found guilty of wilful murder. Garry could only say in court, 'I never did it, that is all I have to say.'

The hanging was Marwood's last execution, and applications poured in from the public to take up his job, including a letter from a semi-literate man who wrote, 'hopin you will give me a erly hanging for which yu will be responsible…'.

99

MAJOR STRESS FOR THE HANGMAN

Mary Lefley, 26 May 1884

Sixteen years after the Biggadike case, in the village of Wrangle, we have a strangely parallel story: Mary Lefley, aged forty-nine, and her husband William, a cottager aged fifty-nine, were living in a freehold property and reasonably happy, at least on the surface. On 6 February 1884, various friends called at their cottage and all seemed normal, but Mary had set off for Boston, as she often did, to sell produce, and later in the day, around three o'clock, William arrived at the home of the local medical man, Dr Bubb. Lefley was extremely ill and the doctor was not there. He staggered in and hit the floor, retching and moaning. He managed to produce a bowl of rice pudding and told some women present that the food had poison in it.

When he was told again that Dr Bubb was not at home, he said, 'That won't do. I want to see him in one minute, I'm dying fast.' A Dr Faskally (the locum) then came and examined him; it was a desperate situation and the doctor had Lefley carried to his own home, where he died.

When Mary came home that evening her behaviour was confused and, to some, irrational, and that was to have serious repercussions later on. She actually stated to the doctor that she expected Lefley to claim that he had been poisoned. What was reported about her then is strange indeed. A neighbour, Mrs Longden, offered to make Mary some tea, and was told, 'I've had nothing all day because I felt so queer.' Then she talked about making the pudding: 'He told me not to make a pudding as there was plenty cooked, but I said I always make a pudding and would do so as usual.' In themselves, these two statements are quite innocuous, but in the context of the later trial, they were to prove lethal for her.

Other witnesses talked of Mary's references to her husband's attempts at taking his own life. She said, 'It's his badness. He's been a brute since Christmas...'. Then she added that one day recently he had gone out with the intention of hanging himself. Mary, when questioned about this, said that she had not followed him into the yard after he had said he was to take his life. But odd though this was, the focus was really on the poison and no one could explain where it had come from. A screwed-up piece of paper was found with white powder, but it proved not to be arsenic. These patterns of behaviour have all the hallmarks of a couple with profound problems in their relationship and in their personal sense of identity and well-being. Mary had even described, in a convoluted way, an experience on the wagon going to Boston that suggested she was under mental strain. She had explained that she had forgotten why she was going, and had a deep sense of confusion.

At Lincoln Assizes, on 7 May, she was in the box; there was no other suspect. Police had been convinced there had been foul play and she was the obvious target. She had been charged on circumstantial evidence only. She pleaded not guilty, and then had to listen to an astounding piece of medical information from the post-mortem. There had been a massive amount of arsenic in the rice pudding: over 135 grains. A fatal dose would only have been two grains. Despite the fact that the white powder found in her home was shown to be harmless, witnesses were called and the trial proceeded. The strangest testimony came from William's nephew William Lister, who recounted an argument between the couple on 1 February, when his uncle had been drinking a great deal of ale. Uncle William came to his nephew's bed in the night and told him that he had just attempted suicide.

Other witnesses had heard Mary say that she wished her husband was 'dead and out of the way.' It was going to be a tough challenge for the defence and the best they could do was take up the data regarding the man's attempted suicide and show this his death was a successful suicide. But the judge had noted the strange, indifferent behaviour of Mary at the time her husband was dying and thought it very odd that she did not go to the man's bedside when his death was inevitable.

When sentenced to death, her reply was, 'I'm not guilty, and I never poisoned anyone in my life.' Patrick Wilson, writing in 1971, makes a strong case for her innocence and lists eleven anomalies in the investigation, all pointing to the irrationality of the judgement. The main objections are that William must have noticed the taste of such a massive amount of arsenic in the pudding, and also that there was no evidence of a motive, with the related points about there being no evidence that they had a deeply unhappy marriage.

There is also a great deal of helpful detail in the memoirs of the hangman. James Berry was aware that William Lefley was something of a simpleton, that he worked as a

*James Berry, who
hanged Mary Lefley.
(Author's collection)*

carrier, and his approach to business made him some enemies as well as men who would ridicule him. These were factors that never came up at Mary's trial, and Berry, new to the job and keen to do things right, thought he was about to hang an innocent woman. But he was a professional, with a task ahead of him and he carried on. He wrote his own account of the process in his memoirs:

> To the very last she protested her innocence, though the night before she was very restless and constantly exclaimed, 'Lord, Thou knowest all!' She would have no breakfast and when I approached her she was in a nervous agitated state, praying to God for salvation... but as an innocent woman... she had to be led to the scaffold by two female warders.

Berry records that Mary, when he went to fetch her on the fateful morning, was ill. She also shouted, 'Murder!' Berry wrote with feeling and some repugnance about the whole business. He noted that her cries as she was dragged along to the scaffold were piercing. As Berry reported, 'Our eyes were downcast, our sense numbed, and down the cheeks of some the tears were rolling.' After all, as soon as Berry arrived at the gaol, a female warder told him, 'She has never ceased to protest her innocence. Oh, Mr Berry, I am sure as I can be that she never committed that dreadful crime. You have only to talk to the woman to know that...'. Berry noted that on arrival he 'found the gaol in a state of panic', and, later, the chaplain's prayers had sounded 'more like a sob'.

The final irony is the troubling parallel to Biggadike's tale, if we believe James Berry, because he relates that a farmer, who had been humiliated by Lefley, confessed to the poisoning on his deathbed. He claimed to have crept into the cottage that day and put the poison in the pudding.

100

FISHERMAN WITH A GUN

Richard Insole, 21 February 1887

Mr Justice Field, a judge on the Midland Circuit, arrived in Lincoln for the assizes in 1887 fresh from a number of murder trials. He was well known for his tough, no-nonsense attitude, and now he was to preside over the trial of a Grimsby man. He was then aged seventy-four, but a long life had certainly not softened his character; in fact he had not been called to the Bar until he was thirty-seven and it could be said that he was determined to make his mark. In his long career he was involved in several high-profile cases and the small matter of yet another working man who murdered his wife was not going to trouble him.

Mr Harris, defending the accused, Richard Insole, knew that he had a difficult task. It was an uncomplicated case. Insole, a fisherman, had been separated from his wife, Sarah, since July the previous year; she had gone back to live with her parents and was earning a wage. Insole had a set intention to take her life; such was his hatred of her. He bought a revolver and cartridges on 7 January 1887 and, at around ten in the morning, he appeared at Sarah's parents' home. He went in and started a row.

The couple had a furious interchange and eventually Insole fired a shot at his wife, but she managed to knock his hand so that the bullet went high and wide of her. But the man was determined and he shot again, this time hitting her in the chest and she fell back into a chair. He was still not finished, and fired again, but this time deciding to fire into the floor instead. Still in a rage, he was interrupted by the arrival of his wife's mother, whom he shoved roughly away before putting the barrel of the gun next to Sarah's heart and firing twice. She died instantly, of course, and Insole ran off. He was tracked down without any difficulty at his own home, where he was arrested and detained.

His defence lawyer argued that Insole had been desperately jealous and in that state had been totally distracted and not at all his normal self. As The Times reported on the case, Mr Harris had admitted defeat, and had said that 'he could not contend that there were any circumstances which would reduce the offence to manslaughter' and that he still thought that the introduction of the notion of jealousy would help the jury see his client in 'a favourable light'. He was backing a loser. Yet it must be recorded that Harris's speech achieved one thing: it guided the jury to suggest a recommendation for mercy after a guilty verdict. They had been convinced by the account of Sarah's affair with another man. The jury had actually used the word 'provocation' when they asked for mercy. In 1887 that was a word with no weight at all in a case where a killer had planned to intentionally take a life. He bought the gun and bullets, went to Sarah's home, roughly assaulted her mother, and fired the gun with a definite intention to kill. The death sentence was passed on him and Justice Field repeated the recommendation to mercy, but it was, as he well knew, futile.

In Grimsby, however, a sufficiently large number of people felt that they should sign a petition to save Insole's life. On 12 February, it was noted in the newspapers: 'A petition is being signed that the capital sentence passed upon Richard Insole, the Grimsby murderer, be commuted to penal servitude for life.' It was fruitless and on Monday 21 February, at the new prison on Greetwell Road, Lincoln, the Bradford executioner James Berry arrived to see Insole into the next world.

In Berry's memoirs, in which many of his victims were given a few pages of detail regarding their exits, it is noticeable that Richard Insole had no more than a few basic words. He must have formed an opinion of the killer so low that he took a certain pleasure in hanging Insole that day in Lincoln.

James Berry had another appointment the next day, in Nottingham, where another young wife-killer was waiting to step up to the scaffold and the very professionally prepared noose. This was Benjamin Terry – a man sentenced by Mr Justice Field, who was so accustomed to putting on the black cap that one more Grimsby fisherman was just another face before him who deserved to die.

101

A SHOOTING AT WATERSIDE

Arthur Spencer, 28 July 1891

Arthur Spencer, a butcher from Nottinghamshire, arrived in Lincoln and took up lodgings with Mary Garner in Chelmsford Street. Even after leaving there, he still returned; he was feeling attracted to Garner and he wanted to return, but the situation was becoming one

Waterside; one of its more atmospheric stretches. (*Author's collection*)

of harassment. He even asked her to marry him but was rejected. His response was to say, 'If I don't have you, no other man shall. I shall shoot you and myself too.' She was not impressed, and thought he was fooling around when he later came back with a gun in his hand. She made it quite clear she never wanted to see him again.

Spencer was incited to act on his vow. He came again to her house, and was asked if he had the 'pop gun' with him. He still had possessions there so he went upstairs for them and was gone some time, so Mary Garner went up to him. Then shots were heard and Garner's son heard her shout, 'Oh my God!' The alarm was raised. Garner was not yet dead, but calling for help. A doctor was called but she died later that day. Spencer, true to his promise, was in the bedroom, having tried to take his own life.

Spencer had a bullet in his skull, so his trial was delayed; but when he finally appeared in court there was no defence. He was only twenty-two, and there was some feeling against hanging one so young, but hang he did, at the hands of James Berry.

102

CIGARS IN THE DEATH CELL

Henry Rumbold, 19 December 1893

This is the tale of a Grimsby mariner who, while awaiting execution in Lincoln Prison, decided to confess to an entirely separate crime to the one he was in the execution cell for: ramming and sinking the fishing boat of a company with which he was in direct competition. He had never said anything about this to anyone and had been well paid for the ruthless job.

Thirty-seven-year-old Henry Rumbold was the captain of a fishing smack working from Grimsby. He was married but was fond of female company, which was not hard to find around the docks. He started spending time with a woman thirteen years his junior, Harriet Rushby.

Henry convinced Harriet that, if she were to be available to him when he was back from sea, that she would be well housed and looked after. He provided her with somewhere to lodge, but it wasn't enough for her. The exciting pull of the pubs and the musical entertainment was too much. She also liked spending time with a variety of men: she was young and men were attracted to her. When Henry came home from sea and went to visit her, Harriet was nowhere to be found.

This is a tale of possession. Rumbold perhaps thought that a man with some kind of status in the community should have a mistress, and a decent one at that. When she didn't turn out to be the woman he wanted he took it into his head to go looking for her, and with a gun in his hand. Rumbold searched the streets, working his way through noisy drunks and street brawls, and eventually found her in one of the night-time crowds. He had the gun out and was in a rage; she was grabbed and taken to the upstairs room of her lodging house. Rumbold yelled for the other hangers-on to keep their distance. No one felt brave enough to try to protect her.

The crowd outside heard Harriet cry out, 'Don't murder me Harry, in my sins!' and a gunshot rang out. Rumbold then coolly stepped outside and walked away into the night, blood visible on his hand. But Rumbold was not concerned with witnesses. He was a man on the edge of reason and he knew that the only thing left for him was to end his life, but he claimed later at the trial that his weapon had malfunctioned when he tried to shoot himself in the head. In desperation, he walked to the nearest police officer and confessed.

In the dock at Lincoln, Rumbold listened while the tale of his lavish spending on the young woman was related. He had treated her very well but had snapped when she turned out to be a disappointment to him. There was an attempt at claiming manslaughter, but this flimsy excuse was rejected and Rumbold was charged with murder. His response was that it was right that he should die. 'Of course I killed her,' he said, 'and I hope when I die I shall join the girl I shot.'

Before the black cap was placed on the judge's head, Rumbold was asked if he wished to speak. He then made a strange request: he asked for a supply of cigars enough to last him for his last three weeks of life in Lincoln Prison. The judge indulged him and let it happen.

Rumbold smoked himself into a state of agitation, no doubt, before he walked to the scaffold on 19 December 1893, where James Billington was waiting to stretch his neck. Perhaps Henry was fortunate in having Billington, for the hangman had worked on reducing the time spent pinioning his victims from minutes down to just a few seconds. The hangman with the nickname 'Jimmy Armhole' would help Rumbold to leave this life speedily.

What about his other adventure on the wrong side of the law? Henry Rumbold (called Rumbell in the report) had been involved in a case in which a smack called the *Fortuna* belonging to an alderman of Grimsby, Henry Smethurst, had been rammed and sunk by the *Ibis* after a collision. The claim was that the collision had been caused by Henry, who was master of the *Ibis*, and they also said, as *The Times* reported, that 'the plaintiff Smethurst had incited and procured Rumbell to sink the *Fortuna*.'

Whatever the truth of the matter, Henry was certainly a man not to be crossed and his temper was destined to lead him to the gallows, the killer's destination after he stubbed out the last of his cigars.

The black cap is on: Judge Hawkins about to pass sentence. (Author's collection)

103

'SHE WON'T AGGRAVATE ME ANY MORE!'

Joseph Bowser, 27 July 1897

Joseph Bowser was a farmer from Donington, a respected man who worked as a poor law guardian and an overseer of the poor. His wife, Susan, had been married before and had a son who lived with them in Lincoln. Bowser had a problem with anger management: when he got angry there was trouble. He also liked a few drinks and Susan would join him in that habit, but he often became violent towards her.

One day, some of Bowser's relatives visited, and they talked to Susan, knowing that Bowser was upstairs, asleep and full of whisky. Later on the visitors went for a walk, at which point Bowser emerged from the bedroom, and came downstairs with a loaded gun. He kicked his wife and threw her into the yard. A servant girl saw this, and ran to help Susan. When the visitors arrived back, they saw the farmer with the shotgun and heard him say, 'I shall shoot her and she won't aggravate me any more!' He fired once and missed, but fired again and smashed Susan's skull.

In court, it was pointed out that Susan also had a temper and a drink problem, and there was an effort to prove Bowser insane, but in only ten minutes the jury found him guilty of murder.

Bowser was a big man; he weighed in at seventeen stones when hangman James Billington saw him into eternity.

104

MURDER BY RAT POISON

Edward Bell, 25 July 1899

Edward Bell managed to poison his wife, Mary, without being detected by the authorities; and even his live-in mother-in-law did not suspect him. This was because the railwayman, who had a lover and wanted rid of his wife, had at first administered rat poison to her and then strychnine, telling her that it was medicine from the doctor, so both wife and mother-in-law thought it was acceptable to drink. Of course, Mary died in agony.

Mary had found out about Bell's affair, and there was violence between the two and even a threat from Mary to take her own life. The statement made about him at trial sums up the situation: 'Love for his wife, for their children even, was dead in him. A sense of honour had perished long ago. With his passion for the girl on the one hand and his irritation at the marriage bonds on the other, it reached a crisis…'.

Mary's mother thought her daughter had died from some natural illness, but in the end it was Bell's guilty conscience that got the better of him and he wrote a confession: 'I cannot keep it no longer. The doctor never sent that powder and I am miserable about it.' Mary's body was exhumed and a post-mortem revealed the presence of the poison in her.

In just two minutes, Bell was found guilty at Lincoln. The hanging was an exceptional case as James Billington, the hangman, was ill, and sent his son, William, in his place. He was allowed to proceed.

105

GRIMSBY KNIFE MURDER

Samuel Smith, 10 March 1903

Samuel Smith and Lucy Lingard were both very drunk on 18 November 1902. Smith was forty-five and Lucy thirty-three; they both lived away from their spouses and Smith tended to live with Lucy and her four children whenever he happened to be home from the sea. He was a Devonian sailor who had befriended Lucy and her husband, and he used to drop in and eat with them from time to time. When Lucy left her husband, the two grew close.

They moved into Fourth Terrace, Hope Street, and life should have been brighter for Lucy, but Samuel was a man with a bad temper and he could be very unstable. That black day in November they had both been on a drinking binge all afternoon and when they went home they took a quart of ale with them: not a smart move when they had been arguing for hours and there was a rage simmering in Smith. Lucy's eldest daughter, Rose, was in the room when Smith began to lose control. He hit Lucy in the face, giving her a black eye. Lucy decided to go to bed and leave him to brood.

At that point, two neighbours, women named Martin and Summerfield, came to talk to her. They seem to have been aware of the trouble and, of course, the black eye was the focus of their conversation. The women were very supportive and in fact took it upon themselves to give Smith a ticking off for doing such an awful thing to a woman. He did manage to apologise so all must have seemed well to them when they left the couple in the house.

They left late, at around 11 p.m., but not long after they heard a scream. Someone else on the street, a Mrs Ward, was quickly on the scene and saw Smith standing over his wife's body, moving to a chair when Ward arrived. Rose had also raised the alarm, racing out into the street to shout for a policeman. It was clear that Lucy had tried in vain to protect herself but she was savagely wounded, having been stabbed eleven times – in the head, face, chest and arms. She died in hospital four days later. It transpired that Smith had seen that she was in agony when he stepped away from her, then took up the knife again and renewed the attack.

There was a feeling in some quarters that if both were drunk, then blame might be hard to apportion, particularly as it was a common opinion that Smith was 'feeble-minded'. But he had killed her brutally and the verdict of wilful murder was not difficult to arrive at.

When he was sentenced to death the townsfolk began to take more interest in the crime and a petition was raised. It was destined to be a futile act, however.

Smith is on record as having said that Lucy was not at all to blame and that there had been nothing to provoke him on her part; he had killed her in a rage and thrown the knife into the fireplace. Mr Justice Kennedy at Lincoln Assizes had no alternative but to sentence Smith to be hanged. He was to become a client of hangman William Billington, and he left this life at Lincoln Prison on 10 March 1903.

Throughout the Victorian period, there had been repeated attempts to make out that intoxication might be categorised as a defence in murder trials, but the very best lawyers in the land had failed to give that any substance, so there was no point in Smith's defence, led by Mr Binner, even contemplating such a thing. A defence concerning his 'feeble-mindedness' also never materialised into anything. To local people the case was about a fight between two drunks – but there is no doubt that poor Lucy carries no blame at all for the terrible way her life was taken from her.

106

BOULTHAM MURDER

Leonard Patchett, 28 July 1903

Leonard Patchett, just twenty-six in 1903, married a woman whose first husband had taken his own life. Sadly, her second husband was a jealous, edgy and bad-tempered man. Sarah was five years older than he, and they settled down to married life with several problems, the worst of which was his drinking habits.

The couple had a daughter together, and that event had the potential to change things for the better, but it did not. Tired of his bad temper and drinking, Sarah took a job as live-in housekeeper to a man named King in Spencer Street, Lincoln. The couple spent a final week together at Shirebrook; nothing had been worked out between them and when Sarah told him that they had no future, Patchett, believing his wife was being unfaithful, vowed to follow and kill her. Sarah thought his words were simply fired by alcohol.

Patchett took a job as a bricklayer in Gainsborough. He would loiter around the house and accuse Mr King and his wife of all kinds of deviant behaviour. Eventually, he hatched a plan to end the whole relationship in the quickest way: he would kill Sarah.

There was nothing secretive about the plan: he had been staying with his sister in Gainsborough and one day he took a train to Lincoln. Stopping off at a shop, he bought a new collar and said to the assistant, 'I'm about to do something I've never done before... if you buy the *Lincolnshire Echo* you will see!' He had arranged to meet and talk with Sarah about the situation and they met in Boultham Park. They were seen walking in Boultham Lane. To people passing by they would have seemed like any other courting couple taking a stroll. But in fact, Patchett strangled her and left her body on a manure heap. Her body was found three days later.

Again, Patchett could not resist telling the world what he had done. He told two people the day after the killing that he had 'done murder'. He even told a roommate that he had killed someone. When he was arrested and later in court, all he could argue in defence, in sheer desperation, was that he had an alibi – that he was on the train to Gainsborough when the murder took place. It didn't take a genius to prove him wrong; a glance at the railway timetable resolved that. In addition to this, two men had seen him in Boultham Lane at around 8 p.m., the time he claimed he was waiting to catch a train in the city. He confessed that he had choked his wife with a handkerchief. Now, William Billington was waiting to tie something around Patchett's neck. He was hanged on 28 July 1903.

107

BATTERED BY A COAL HAMMER

William Duddles, 20 November 1907

William Duddles lodged at Lutton Marsh, at the home of Mr and Mrs Gear. But in October 1907 he tried to stab the man of the house and was thrown out. It was a stormy relationship; he was taken back in again and was offensive, but beer was bought and all three sat down together. When Gear left later on to fetch more ale, neighbours heard noises coming from the house.

When Gear returned home he found his wife's body lying in a pool of blood, a coal hammer lying by the corpse. He saw Duddles running away. In court for the coroner's hearing, a verdict of wilful murder was returned and Duddles was accused. He was arrested and soon, at Lincoln, Mr Commissioner Atkinson gave the death sentence but with a recommendation for mercy from the jury, which did not come. He was hanged by the first of the Pierrepoint hangmen dynasty, Henry.

108

CALM WITH THE HANGMAN

William Wright, 10 March 1920

In 1920 the *Lincoln Gazette* reported that William Wright, an ex-soldier, had been executed at Lincoln Prison. He had murdered his sweetheart, Annie Coulbeck, who was pregnant with their child, in Caistor. The report stated: 'To Canon Scott, the prison chaplain, he said this morning that he intended killing his victim, and he acknowledged the justice of his sentence, but so far as is known, he has shown no repentance for the deed.'

Wright had been sitting in the taproom of the Talbot Hotel in Caistor when he had said to a chimneysweep there: 'Sweep, three weeks rope! Black cap! Hanged by the neck! Finish!' Someone calling to see Annie Coulbeck later that night found her body on the kitchen floor. Wright said that he and Annie had quarrelled over a brooch she was wearing, and Wright had said it was from 'one of her fancy men.' He strangled her and went home.

There was a defence of insanity, as there had been a long history of mental illness in Wright's family; but even his army record had no effect in the defence statements. As he had made a lucid and exact confession when questioned after the murder, it was stated that he was in full possession of his faculties when he had killed Annie. He was found guilty and hanged by Thomas Pierrepoint.

109

INSANITY PLEAS FAIL

Frank Fowler & George Robinson, 13 December 1922

A young woman lay dead on the floor of the White Horse Hotel in Market Deeping in September 1922; she was just two months short of her nineteenth birthday. She was Mrs Ivy Prentice, and her mother, a widow, was soon to marry again. She had been enjoying looking at her mother's wedding presents in the hotel when Frank Fowler, a thirty-five-year-old farm manager, came in the front door with a double-barrelled shotgun in his hands. He had been drinking in the pub earlier, and had left by the back door. Anyone observing him would have put two and two together and expected a broodiness and dissatisfaction in him that night: he had been drinking alone and slipped out to get the gun. There was no problem about ascertaining any malice aforethought in this case. Fowler knew exactly who he was gunning for: his murderous thoughts were focused on young Ivy and he shot her in the chest. She fell down by the feet of her mother and their friends.

The White Horse. (Courtesy of Lincolnshire Archives)

There was then an incredible act of courage on the part of the girl's mother, Edith D'Arcy, who was manager of the pub. She lunged at the gunman as he was aiming to fire again, at her. The gun was pushed to one side and a shot was fired through the window. This all happened in a private room, but the customers in the saloon bar heard the shot and rushed in; in no time the gunman was overhauled and held fast by the crowd. The law, in the shape of Sergeant Bennett, soon arrived.

A doctor was summoned and pronounced Ivy Prentice dead not long after. It was a mystery when it came to trying to come up with a motive for this murder; Frank Fowler was a family friend, and as the *Lincolnshire, Boston and Spalding Free Press* reported, he had given a 'present of a substantial character on the occasion of a recent wedding in the family.'

Ivy's mother, in spite of the traumatic nature of this horrible event, went ahead with her wedding and married William Kitchener. Following hard on their marriage was the inquest, and Fowler was then charged at Bourne police station. Mrs Kitchener (*née* D'Arcy) said that she had been showing some presents to friends by the table when the killer came in. She recalled her other daughter, Gertrude, shouting, 'Bring a light, Ivy has been shot!' It was a terrible scene, as they were in semi-darkness, and only when the room was lit did she see and feel the blood on a chair.

The search for a motive went no further than the obvious: Fowler was jealous of the young woman's husband, George. His words are recalled, spoken as he was grabbed in the pub, with his victim lying dead a few feet away; 'I have had my bloody revenge.' Ivy's mother could not think of any instance when her daughter might have given Fowler cause to have such a hatred of her. On the contrary, Fowler's burning rancour was expressed in bizarre ways: some time earlier he had faced George Prentice in a bar and hissed at him; then he had returned, taken his hat off and said, 'How is that for a bloody haircut? I will have my own back on you one day, you bugger!' He had been behaving strangely for some time, but he knew exactly what he was doing that night in the White Horse Hotel when he took the girl's life.

Fowler pleaded not guilty at Lincoln Assizes, but there was no defence and no question of any other offence than murder with an intention to kill aforethought. Mr Justice Lush had no doubt that he had to place the black cap on his wig and pronounce a sentence of death. Frank Fowler was hanged at Lincoln Prison on 13 December 1922, along with George Robinson, who had cut Frances Pacey's throat at Dorrington.

110

KILLED FOR A BUNGALOW

Bertram Kirby, 4 January 1928

Bertram and Minnie Kirby lived with their young son in a bungalow in Louth. Their two other grown-up children lived elsewhere, one in Louth and one in Canada. Their lives must have seemed ordinary and happy to neighbours, particularly on the morning of 18 July 1927, when Bertram was seen waving goodbye to his family. But Bertram called at his son Harry's lodgings in Louth and asked the landlady there to look after his younger son, as he and his wife would be away for a while. He was carrying a suitcase and said he was going to Grimsby.

Kirby had a cunning plan; he told people he had sold the bungalow and he started selling clothes. Then his son, Harry, reported to the police that he could not gain entry to the bungalow, and an entry was forced by police. There they found Mrs Kirby's body; she had been attacked with an axe, and there were letters which suggested a planned suicide pact. But of course they may have been an elaborate attempt by Bertram to cover up the killing.

Bertram Kirby was the subject of a determined police search and was eventually found and charged. When he was told that he was wanted with reference to his wife's death he said, 'All right, I'm not going to cause you any trouble. By God boy, you don't know what things are. I hope you never will. You don't know what I've had to put up with.'

He was tried in Lincoln before Mr Justice Swift, where the defence pleaded insanity, largely because, whilst in the army, Kirby had twice tried to take his own life. There was a clear motive for the killing: his small business had failed and he was desperate for money. His wife owned the bungalow, and he thought that he would inherit it if she died. Kirby was sentenced to death.

Thomas Pierrepoint led him to the scaffold after a final night on earth in which he barely slept. As he was pinioned on the gallows he seemed to be resigned to his death.

111

THE MURDER OF
MONA TINSLEY

Frederick Nodder, 30 December 1937

Missing from her home... at 11, Thoresby Avenue, Newark, since Tuesday, 5 January, 1937, Mona Lilian Tinsley, aged 10 years (rather short for age), dark hair (bobbed with fringe) rosy cheeks, four prominent teeth at front... It has been established that this girl was seen at Hayton Smeath, near Retford at about midday on Wednesday, 6 January, 1937.

(Text from a police poster)

Lorry driver Frederick Nodder moved into new lodgings in Newark in 1935, where his landlady was Mrs Tinsley. He didn't stay long, but he made a mark with the children. To them he was 'Uncle Fred.' He was clearly a man who was difficult to live with, at least in the adult world. When he later moved on to East Retford, he proved to be a handful for the landlady, with his bad habits and tendency to create a mess.

But back in Newark, the large Tinsley family was now one short of the usual number. Mona, aged ten, was missing. Her father, Wilfred, was frantic with worry. When Mona did not return home from school on 5 January 1937, the search began. Her school was not far away and Wilfred began his search there. The police were called and a description went out: she was wearing a knitted suit and Wellingtons. A boy named Willie Placket recalled seeing Mona talking to a man and said that he would recognise the man if he saw him again. A Mrs Hird had also seen Mona with a man 'who was a lodger with the girl's mother' – she recognised his hook nose and ginger moustache. A bus conductor also recalled seeing him. The net was closing in on the person described as 'a man with staring eyes.'

The police traced Nodder to Retford where he was picked up. He had been living under the name Hudson, and was the father of a child living locally. Mona had been seen with 'Uncle Fred' and consequently, as Mona was now officially missing, Nodder was interviewed. His story was that he had given the girl a lift to Sheffield, and then put Mona on a bus to her aunt's in Worksop. It was all highly suspicious and he was arrested for abduction. There was no body, so there was no murder charge. In court, the abduction still stood and he was sent to prison. While he was in custody, a massive search for Mona began; 1,000 people joined in to search areas between Retford and Newark. It was such a wide area that police from Nottinghamshire, Lincolnshire and Derbyshire forces all spent time and manpower on the case. Scotland Yard sent men to step up the campaign: the Chesterfield Canal was dragged.

Nodder had been tried at Birmingham, but now off he went to Nottingham to face a murder charge. So began Frederick Nodder's period inside the walls of Lincoln Prison. Three months after his trial, Mona's body was found in the River Idle, close to Bawtry. She had been strangled. Nodder was in court again, but nothing he could say did him any good. The presiding judge, Mr Justice Macnaughton, said, 'Justice has slowly, but surely, overtaken you and it only remains for me to pronounce the sentence which the law and justice require...'

The treat barrister, Norman Birkett, had spoken for the prosecution; it was to be his last trial, appearing for the Crown. It was a terrible case, and aroused a widespread sense of outrage, as Nodder had sexually assaulted Mona before killing her. It took five minutes for her to die. 'Uncle Fred' had turned out to be a monster. Photos of him show a man with

Norman Birkett. (Author's collection)

Frederick Nodder.
(Drawing by Laura Carter)

a matching flat cap and scarf of small check pattern and a thick overcoat. His eyes are piercing and he shows a face to the world that expresses nothing substantial. 'Something is missing in him', is a phrase often said of these types of killers.

He was sentenced to hang. A few days after Christmas, 1937, he was in the hands of the hangman and left this world. He was hanged in Lincoln Prison on Greetwell Road, and his last moments would have been on the wing of the execution suite. He would have fallen through the trap to dangle and die – very quickly – taking less time to die than his victim had done. The corpse was taken down and buried with quicklime, as was the custom. But was that the last to be seen of Frederick Nodder inside the prison walls? Some think not.

The staff have reported sightings of a man walking the corridors, wearing a dark overcoat and flat check cap. One warden turned a corner to see a strange man with piercing eyes coming towards him. Some have merely glimpsed his profile, with the distinctive hooked nose and ginger moustache.

If the tales are true, then this evil man is as restless now as he was in life. In fairly recent times, when building work was carried out at the prison site, the graves of executed prisoners were taken up and carried to the city cemetery. The more serious ghost hunters date the appearances of the ghost of Uncle Fred to that time. The man with the staring eyes, if he exists in spirit form, will still try his hardest to unsettle the unwary night-walker. Nodder was always a man who haunted, loitered, and watched people.

112

MURDER AT WALESBY

Leonard Holmes, 28 May 1946

Leonard Holmes lived with his wife in Walesby, Nottinghamshire, and worked as a lorry driver. He served in the army during the Second World War and was based at Huddersfield, where he started an affair with a Mrs Shaw. When he was demobbed in 1945, he told Mrs Shaw that they could now be together, for he had killed his wife. But the body was found and he was arrested at Retford railway station.

His explanation of what had happened was that he had argued with his wife at the Carpenter's Arms near their home because his wife was flirting with two airmen. She confessed that she had been unfaithful and openly said that she did not trust him either. Holmes claimed that he had attacked her with a hammer on the spur of the moment, not after premeditation. But he had then strangled her, and thus could not plead manslaughter.

At the trial it was stated that he had sent a telegram to Mrs Shaw saying, 'See you Sunday or Monday for sure. Be prepared. Ok. All fixed. Len.' There was no provocation allowed and the judge directed the jury to be sure of that, so manslaughter was going to be hard to prove. There was an appeal but the verdict of guilty was upheld and Holmes was hanged by Thomas Pierrepoint on 28 May 1946.

113

MURDER IN A BORSTAL

Kenneth Strickson, 22 March 1949

Irene Phillips was matron at the Sherwood Borstal in Nottingham, and was also the person who changed the accoutrements in the prison chapel. On 19 November 1948 staff found the door locked and were shocked to find blood coming out from under the door of the vestry. Kenneth Strickson, who was just twenty-one, was trying to go out of the gate to join a builder's party but had no pass. When he couldn't obtain one, he said, 'I think I have killed the matron.'

Irene had been savagely attacked: she had been struck with a smashed chair and her skull had been crushed, causing brain damage. The story that emerged was that Strickson had made advances toward the matron, even telling other prisoners, 'I'm going up to the chapel with matron and I'm going to have a go at her there. I'm going to see what I can get out of her.' He even said that if she fought him he would 'cosh her on the head.' There was no substance in an insanity claim and he was condemned to die. Albert Pierrepoint officiated.

114

THE PERFECT MURDER GOES WRONG

Herbert Leonard Mills, 11 December 1951

In a stretch of rough ground known as 'The Jungle' in Sherwood Vale, the body of Mrs Mabel Tattershaw was found in August 1951 after a phone call to the *News of the World* newspaper was made by Herbert Leonard Mills. He claimed that he had gone there to read poetry and had found her body. Clearly, Mills was expecting to make some money from the paper, and a journalist named Norman Rae invited him to a meeting in Nottingham on 24 August. There, Mills confessed to the murder and accepted £80 from Rae. He claimed that he had courted Mabel, had agreed to meet her at 'The Jungle', where he had beaten and then strangled her to death. He said that he had wanted to commit the perfect murder.

He was arrested and charged, and appeared at Nottingham assizes on 19 November 1951. There he changed his tale, saying that he had rebuffed the woman's advances and that later on he had found her body. As he never denied the fact that he had met her, forensic work was a challenge, but the jury accepted the details of a murder charge and he was sentenced to death. There was no reprieve, and he was hanged on 11 December 1951.

115

STABBED TO DEATH

Eric Norcliffe, 12 December 1952

In June 1952, neighbours heard cries and shouts from the home of Eric and Kathleen Norcliffe at Hammerwater Drive, Warsop. Someone heard the woman cry, 'Oh Eric, what are you doing?' When police arrived they found Kathleen stabbed to death in the kitchen and Eric wounded in the arm. He told officers that he had emptied the gas meter of its money and that when Kathleen had discovered this – when the meter man had come for payment – they had a savage row.

The trial was loaded with statements about Eric's sanity – or lack of it. Various opinions were given, but it was ascertained that he had killed Kathleen intentionally. Although he had been suffering from depression, the defence of insanity was rejected and he was sentenced to die. His only words were, 'As far as I can see, the only thing this court has been concerned with is where and when I did it. No one seems bothered why I did it.' He was duly hanged.

116

NO CASE OF SELF-DEFENCE

Harold Fowler, 12 August 1954

Doreen Mulligan was already married when she met Harold Fowler in 1952. They became close and soon began an affair. When Mr Mulligan found out, there was a quarrel, and the pregnant Doreen left her husband to live with Fowler. After the birth of her son, and after living with her sister for a while, Doreen started a new life with Fowler. All might have been well, but Mulligan was not finished with her yet.

He turned up at the house and asked for their marriage certificate and a photograph of their daughter, Linda. But things got out of hand and Mulligan struck Doreen, calling her a fool. This was too much for Fowler, who took out a knife and stabbed Mulligan. When arrested, Fowler was found with the weapon still in his possession – a double-edged knife. At the trial a defence of provocation was put together, stating that Mulligan had been threatening and aggressive towards Fowler, but that did not hold water. The stabbing was seen as a deliberate and intended attack, and a murder verdict was reached. An appeal for a reprieve failed and Albert Pierrepoint hanged Fowler on 12 August 1954.

117

A BRUTAL KILLING IN SKEGBY

James Robinson, 24 May 1955

In December 1954, Mary Dodsley had tea with a friend but, the next morning, when a neighbour called round to see her, they were met with no response. It was noticed that a window had been broken and left open. The police were called and Mrs Dodsley's body was found: she was eighty-three years old and had been raped and murdered.

A fingerprint expert set to work and a palm print on the broken window led police to James Robinson. He had an alibi – he was drinking in a pub nearby until 10 p.m. – but there was disagreement about the time of death, ranging from nine in the evening to one the next morning.

In spite of doubts regarding the palm print and the time of death, the jury found Robinson guilty and he was sentenced to die, with Albert Pierrepoint again officiating.

118

MURDER IN THE WOODYARD

Kenneth Roberts, 12 July 1955

The facts of the case were straightforward: Kenneth Roberts, a man of twenty-four, married and living in Spencer Avenue, Scunthorpe, telephoned police on the morning of 11 May 1955 to confess to a murder. He had strangled Mary Roberts (no relation) in a woodyard off the Winterton road. He said he had 'gone crazy' and had used the girl's own scarf to strangle her. But the important detail was that he believed her to be already dead when he applied the scarf to her neck.

Inspector Tom Evinson confirmed that Roberts had made the phone call and had led them to the woodyard. He was then remanded and charged with her murder. The focus of the trial was the strangling with the scarf. It was ascertained that he had taken the girl to the yard for sex and, at that point, something in Roberts had snapped. The jury has to decide what the actual cause of death had been – strangulation by the scarf or asphyxiation by hands? They also had to decide whether or not Roberts had intended to kill Mary; was it murder or manslaughter?

At his trial in Nottingham, Roberts was found guilty of murder and hanged at Lincoln by Doncaster hangman Steve Wade. He had not made an appeal and was the last Lincolnshire man to die on the county gallows.

Official confirmation of the hanging of Kenneth Roberts. (Drawing by Laura Carter)

Officers place the notice on the prison door. (Lincolnshire Echo)

119

MURDER OF A WIDOW

John Constantine, 1 September 1960

Lily Parry lived over her shop and always kept the takings in her bedroom at night. A young girl, Judith Reddish, stayed there and on 22 April 1960 she arrived back from an evening out and settled down for the night, then Mrs Parry locked up and went to bed. Early the next day blood was seen coming from under Mrs Parry's bedroom door. The police arrived and found her; her skull broken and almost dead: she died later in hospital.

John Constantine lived in the same street, Waterloo Promenade, Nottingham. His place had a room that was close to the shop and he was duly questioned. He admitted that he had robbed the shop but denied committing murder. He did however say that he had hit out at a figure that advanced towards him. He said at first that he had hit her with a crowbar but changed his story later. He tried to blame someone else, and named another man, Colathan, who was allegedly his accomplice, but Colathan had an alibi, which was confirmed by several people.

The defence brought in the famous 'dog didn't bark' storyline. As Mrs Parry had a dog and it had not barked; they argued that the dog must have been kept silent by an accomplice, but that was not accepted by the jury and they returned a guilty verdict. An appeal failed, and then a reprieve request was turned down. Harry Allen was the executioner, and, as N.V. Gagen has pointed out, there was no high-profile media interest in the execution – only four journalists were present – and no execution notice was posted on the prison gates.

120

LAST MAN ON THE LINCOLN GALLOWS

Wasyl Gnypiuk, 27 January 1961

The man who has the dubious distinction of being the last man to hang in Lincoln was a thirty-four-year-old Polish-Ukrainian who had come to England after the Second World War. Wasyl Gnypiuk suffered from some mental problems and was a heavy drinker, and he killed Louisa Surgey in Worksop on 17 July 1960. The killing was savage in the extreme: he had decapitated her and left her body at an allotment near her home in Ashley Road. Her head was found about a mile away, in a carrier bag.

The killer and the victim knew each other as Louisa had bought her house from the Ukrainian, and they had been friendly for a while. He claimed that he had been very drunk on the night of the murder and had dreamed that he was strangling someone. But any thought of manslaughter was dismissed by the jury when it was learned that he had taken £250 of his victim's money to help pay off some of his debts.

There is one very unusual feature of this last case: there were two stays of execution, and Gnypiuk was the first ever condemned man to appeal to the House of Lords rather than the Home Secretary. His wife had said that her husband had always suffered from terrible nightmares, and the man was clearly a Jekyll and Hyde character, as some people stated at the trial that he was 'kind and gentle'. Harry Allen hanged him on 27 January 1961.

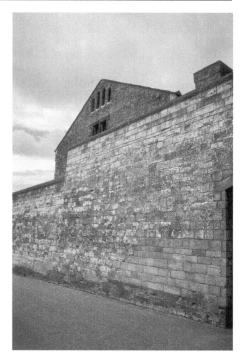

Gaols across the centuries. Clockwise from top left: The Stonebow (Renaissance); the Victorian prison walls; Lincoln Prison, built in 1872. (All author's collection)

APPENDIX

Hangings with little or no information

As stated in the Introduction, there are very few details of hangings before about 1700, with the exception of major cases. Anyone keen to know more about the hangings in the medieval period are referred to the publications of court records by the Lincoln Records Society. The main factors to keep in mind in this context are that, until the fifteenth century, there were all kinds of alternative punishments, mainly outlawry and fines. The medieval kings wanted money, and revenue from felons was very useful in that respect. Outlawry was, in many ways, worse than death. An outlaw lost everything, including his home and family, and had no status in society at all.

The following hangings took place after 1700, but very little is known about the cases:

Date	Name	Crime
March 1716	William Gray	Murder
March 1734	Thomas Worley	Burglary
August 1736	Robert Lidgard	Horse-stealing
March 1737	John Thompson	Burglary
August 1739	Thomas Brown	Robbery
May 1740	William Dykes	Murder
August 1740	John Stovargue	Burglary
March 1741	William Lewin	Burglary
August 1742	Peter Brown & Clay Lee	Sheep-stealing
August 1773	William Moore	Returning from transportation

BIBLIOGRAPHY & SOURCES

BOOKS

Anon, *The Old Bailey Experience* (James Fraser, London, 1833)

Abbott, Geoffrey, *Lipstick on the Noose: Martyrs, Murderers and Madwomen* (Summersdale, 2003)

Boyce, Douglas, *et al.*, *Tudor Market Rasen*, (Market Rasen WEA Branch, Hull, 1985)

Busby, Sian, *The Cruel Mother: A Family Ghost Laid to Rest* (Short Books, London, 2004)

Christoph, J.B., *Capital Punishment and British Politics* (Allen and Unwin, London, 1962)

Crook, G.T., (ed.) *The Complete Newgate Calendar Vol. 3* (Navarre Society, London, 1926)

Cyriax, Oliver, *The Penguin Encyclopaedia of Crime* (Penguin, London, 1996)

Davey, B.J., *Rural Crime in the Eighteenth Century* (University of Hull Press, 1994)

Deans, R. Storry, *Notable Trials: Romances of the Law Courts* (Cassell, London, 1906)

Ellis, John, *Diary of a Hangman* (True Crime Library, Glasgow, 1997)

Evans, Stewart P., *Executioner: The Chronicles of James Berry, Victorian Hangman* (Sutton, Stroud, 2004)

Fielding, Steve, *The Executioner's Bible* (John Blake, London, 2007)

Fielding, Steve, *The Hangman's Record 1868–1899* (Chancery House, London, 1999)

Fisher, H.A., *The History of Kirton in Lindsey* (Spiegel Press, Stamford, 1981)

Friar, Stephen, *The Sutton Companion to Local History* (Sutton, Stroud, 2004)

Gaute, J.H.H. and Odell, Robin, *The Murderers' Who's Who* (Pan, London, 1979)

Gray, Adrian, *Crime and Criminals in Victorian Lincolnshire* (Paul Watkins, Stamford, 1983)

Harrison, J.F.C., *Early Victorian Britain* (Fontana, London, 1988)

Hawkins, Sir Henry, *Reminiscences* (Nelson, London, 1904)

Horn, Pamela, *Labouring Life in the Victorian Countryside* (Sutton, Stroud, 1987)

Jackson, Robert, *The Chief: the Biography of Gordon Hewart, Lord Chief Justice of England, 1922–1940* (Harrap, London, 1959)

Lane, Brian, *The Encyclopaedia of Forensic Science* (Headline, London, 1992)

Neild, Basil, *Farewell to the Assizes: The Sixty-One Towns* (Garnestone, Oxford, 1972)

Porter, Roy, *Madness: A Brief History* (Oxford University Press, Oxford, 2002)

Putwain, David and Sammons, Aidan, *Psychology and Crime* (Routledge, London, 2002)

Rees, Sian, *The Floating Brothel* (Review, London, 2001)

Stallion, Martin and Wall, David S., *The British Police: Police Forces and Chief Officers, 1829–2000* (Police History Society, Hook, 1999)

Taylor, Bernard and Knight, Stephen, *Perfect Murder: A Century of Unsolved Homicides* (Grafton, London, 1988)

Tibballs, Geoff, *The Murder Guide to Great Britain* (Boxtree, London, 1994)

Tobias, J.J., *Crime and Industrial Society in the Nineteenth Century* (Penguin, London, 1967

Walker, Nigel, *Crime and Insanity in England, Vol.1: The Historical Perspective* (Edinburgh University Press, Edinburgh, 1968)

Ward, Jenny, *Crime Busting: Breakthroughs in Forensic Science* (Blandford, London, 1998)

White, William, *History, Gazetteer and Directory of Lincolnshire* (White, Sheffield, 1856)

Wiener, Martin J., *Reconstructing the Criminal: Culture, Law and Policy in England, 1830–1914* (Cambridge University Press, Cambridge, 1990)

Wiener, Martin J., 'Judges *v.* Jurors: Courtroom Tensions in Murder Trials and the Law of Criminal Responsibility in Nineteenth-Century England' (History Cooperative, Fall 1999)

NEWSPAPERS

Lincoln, Rutland and Stamford Mercury 24 December 1847

Lincolnshire Chronicle 19 December 1847

The Times, 29 July 1859

OTHER

Annual Register, 1847

Annual Register, 1831, pp. 51–52 Chronicle

Tales from the Gallows, Lincolnshire Echo (Special Publication, 2001)

Lincolnshire County Council folder, *Convicts of Lincolnshire*, 1988

Other titles published by The History Press

Hanged at York
STEPHEN WADE

This volume gathers together the stories of criminals hanged at York from the middle o the eighteenth century through to the late nineteenth century, when Leeds supersede(York as the main centre of execution. The condemned featured here range from coiner and forgers, to thieves, murderers and highwaymen, the most notorious being Dick Turpin who was hanged on York's Knavesmire in 1739 for horse-stealing. This book will appeal to everyone interested in the shadier side of York's history.

978 0 7509 5042 8

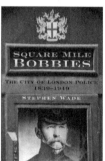

Square Mile Bobbies: The City of London Police 1839–1949
STEPHEN WADE

Between 1839 and 1949, the City of London Police were involved in a succession of majo: national cases, from the attempted assassination of the Rothschilds in 1862 and detectives pursuit of forgers in 1873, to Jack the Ripper's brutal killing of Catherine Eddowes ir 1888 and the notorious siege of Sidney Street in 1911. This chronicle of violent deaths robberies, forgeries and fraudsters is a fascinating look at the social history of the City Police in the chronicles of crime.

978 0 7509 4952 1

Hanged at Durham
STEVE FIELDING

Until hanging was abolished in the 1960s, Durham Gaol was the main centre of execution for convicted killers from all over the North East, and was where seventy-five people took the short walk to the gallows. Steve Fielding's highly readable book features each of these cases, including poisoner Mary Cotton, Carlisle murderer John Vickers, and Gateshead's copy-cat Ripper, William Waddell. Fully illustrated with photographs, news cuttings and engravings, this volume is a must for those interested in Durham's criminal history.

978 0 7509 4750 3

Hanged at Pentonville
STEVE FIELDING

The history of execution at Pentonville began with the hanging of a Scottish hawker in 1902. Over the next sixty years the names of those who made the short walk to the gallows reads like a Who's Who of twentieth-century murder. They include the notorious Dr Crippen, Neville Heath, mass murderer John Christie of Rillington Place, as well a German spies, Italian gangsters, teenage tearaways, cut-throat killers – and many more.

978 0 7509 4950 7

Visit our website and discover thousands of other History Press books.
www.thehistorypress.co.uk